Fit for Business English

Korrespondenz

Robert Tilley

Compact Verlag

Bisher sind in dieser Reihe erschienen:

- Fit for Business English – Telefonieren
- Fit for Business English – Korrespondenz
- Fit for Business English – Verkaufsgespräche
- Fit for Business English – Präsentationen
- Fit for Business English – Geschäftsreisen
- Fit for Business English – Konversation
- Fit for Business English – Redewendungen

Weitere Titel sind in Vorbereitung.

Chefredaktion: Dr. Angela Sendlinger
Redaktion: Gesa Füßle
Fachredaktion: Anthony Moore
Übersetzung: Marc Hillefeld
Produktion: Wolfram Friedrich
Gestaltung: Hendryk Sommer
Titelabbildung: IFA-Bilderteam
Umschlaggestaltung: Axel Ganguin

ISBN 978-3-8174-7772-2
7277721

Besuchen Sie uns im Internet: www.compactverlag.de

Vorwort

Englisch ist die länderübergreifende Sprache der Wirtschaft. Angesichts der zunehmenden Globalisierung der Märkte werden gute Englischkenntnisse immer wichtiger für den beruflichen Erfolg.

Die Reihe **Fit for Business English** ermöglicht dem Benutzer die zielgerechte Vorbereitung auf verschiedene Themenbereiche des modernen Wirtschaftsenglisch.

Der Band **Fit for Business English – Korrespondenz** trainiert speziell die schriftliche Kommunikation im Beruf. Dabei wird gezeigt, wie man in englischer Sprache Geschäftsbriefe, Anfragen, Angebote, Antwortschreiben, Mahnungen, Reklamationen sowie Bewerbungen richtig formuliert.

Dies geschieht anhand einer Story: Der Deutsche Peter Brückner wird von seiner Firma nach England versetzt. Um den nötigen Lernspaß zu garantieren, werden seine Erlebnisse in humorvoller Weise dargestellt.

Alle Dialoge sind praxisnah und sowohl in englischer Sprache als auch in der deutschen Übersetzung angegeben. Die Schlüsselbegriffe sind im Text farbig hervorgehoben.

Nach jedem Dialog folgen zur Überprüfung und Vertiefung des gelernten Wortschatzes kurze Übungen. Die Lösungen sind im Anhang zu finden.

Sprachpraktische und kulturelle Besonderheiten werden an gegebener Stelle angemerkt. Hierzu gehören Tipps zum korrekten Sprachgebrauch sowie landeskundliche Hinweise.

Verschiedene Symbole zu Beginn jedes Abschnitts erleichtern dem Benutzer den Zugriff auf die für ihn relevanten Passagen.

Am Ende jedes Kapitels werden alle wichtigen Vokabeln und Redewendungen nochmals angeführt.

Mit einem abschließenden Test im Anhang kann der Leser seinen Kenntnisstand überprüfen.

Inhalt

Vorwort	3
Story	5
Anfragen	6
Empfehlungen und Reklamationen	36
Angebote	61
Bewerbungsschreiben	86
Antwortschreiben	110
Test	138
Auf einen Blick: Geschäftsbriefe und Redewendungen	141
Glossar	148
Lösungen	153

Here we go: kleine Einleitung am Anfang des Kapitels

Talk Talk Talk: praxisnahe Dialoge mit deutschen Übersetzungen, die wichtigsten Stichwörter sind farbig markiert

Letter: Musterbriefe mit zahlreichen Formulierungen

Train Yourself: abwechslungsreiche Übungen trainieren den gelernten Wortschatz

Background Information: Wissenswertes zu Business und Landeskunde

Do's and Dont's: Tipps zum korrekten Verhalten in Geschäftssituationen

False Friends: Hinweise auf mögliche sprachliche Fehler

Vocabulary: Vokabelliste mit dem Wortschatz des Kapitels

The Test: Im Abschlusstest zeigt es sich: Was haben Sie gelernt? Wo sind vielleicht noch Ihre Schwächen?

Ready to talk: Alles Wichtige zum Nachschlagen

Glossary: Zusammenfassung aller neuen Vokabeln

Solutions: Die Lösungen zu Übungen im Text und zum Abschlusstest

Story

Peter Brückner ist 30 Jahre alt. Nach seinem BWL-Studium wurde er als Assistent des Vertriebsleiters bei der internationalen Firma ERGO Ltd. beschäftigt. ERGO Ltd. ist ein innovatives Unternehmen und hat sich auf die Produktion von Zubehörteilen im IT-Bereich spezialisiert.

Um Peter Brückner auf eine spätere Führungsposition vorzubereiten, wird er in die Filiale nach London versetzt, um dort die Abläufe des internationalen Vertriebs kennen zu lernen. Wie viele andere Unternehmen, legt auch ERGO Ltd. großen Wert darauf, dass künftige Führungskräfte Auslandserfahrungen sammeln.

Dieser Band der Reihe **Fit for Business English** zeigt, wie Peter Brückner die täglich anfallende Geschäftskorrespondenz situationsadäquat und sicher erledigt.
Tatkräftige Unterstützung erhält er dabei von seinen neuen Kollegen, die ihm jederzeit mit nützlichen Tipps zur Seite stehen und ihn auf die kulturellen und sprachlichen Feinheiten hinweisen. Dies sind:

- James Morgan, Managing Director, direkter Vorgesetzter von Peter
- Steve Blackman, Leiter der Verkaufsabteilung
- Melissa Walker, Marketing Managerin
- Lucy Scott, Sekretärin und »gute Seele« des Büros.

Schon bald ist Peter Brückner mit den wichtigsten englischen Redewendungen vertraut und weiß, wie man Geschäftskorrespondenz bearbeitet, Beschwerdebriefe richtig beanwortet, Angebotsschreiben formuliert und Bewerbungsschreiben auswertet.

Anfragen

Requests

Here we go

Die schriftliche Korrespondenz stellt einen wichtigen Teil des Geschäftsalltags dar. Nachdem Peter bisher hauptsächlich damit beschäftigt war, Probleme auf telefonischer Ebene zu lösen, betraut ihn sein Vorgesetzter, James Morgan, nun mit der Aufgabe, sich um seinen persönlichen Postein- und Postausgang zu kümmern. Ein verantwortungsvoller Posten ...

Talk Talk Talk

(The office of James Morgan, Managing Director of ERGO Limited)

(Das Büro von James Morgan, Managing Director von ERGO Limited)

J. Good morning, Peter. Have a good weekend?

J. Guten Morgen, Peter. Wie war Ihr Wochenende?

P. Good morning, Mr Morgan. Fine thanks. I took advantage of the rainy weather and **caught up on some letter-writing**. A lot of my friends in Germany haven't heard from me for some time now.

P. Guten Morgen, Mr Morgan. Danke, gut. Ich habe das Beste aus dem regnerischen Wetter gemacht und **ein paar überfällige Briefe geschrieben**. Viele meiner Freunde in Deutschland haben schon lange nichts mehr von mir gehört.

J. I hope you haven't got **writer's cramp**. And I hope you haven't grown tired of writing letters because that's just what I want you to take over from me this week. During my absence last week the **in-tray** has become full of letters waiting to be answered.

J. Ich hoffe, Sie haben keinen **Schreibkrampf** bekommen. Und ich hoffe, Sie sind des Schreibens dabei noch nicht leid geworden, denn genau das sollen Sie diese Woche für mich übernehmen. Während meiner Abwesenheit letzte Woche hat sich der **Eingangs-**

You know enough now about the business to reply to them for me. Just **dictate** them to Lucy and she'll **type** them **up** for you. When you've completed a **batch** put them in my **out-tray**. There are also some **emails to attend to**. You'll find them in the general ERGO **file**.

korb mit Briefen gefüllt, die darauf warten, beantwortet zu werden. Sie kennen das Geschäft jetzt gut genug, um sie für mich zu beantworten. **Diktieren** Sie sie einfach Lucy und sie wird sie für Sie **abtippen**. Wenn Sie einen **Stoß** fertig haben, legen Sie ihn einfach in meinen **Ausgangskorb**. Es gibt auch noch ein paar **E-Mails, die zu bearbeiten sind**. Sie finden sie im allgemeinen ERGO-**Ordner**.

P. I'll do my best, Mr Morgan. But there are just a few questions of **style** I'd like to sort out first. I'm still a bit uncertain how **to end a letter** in English - there seem to be so many different forms of closing a letter ... .

P. Ich werde mein Bestes tun, Mr Morgan. Ich habe aber noch ein paar Fragen bezüglich des **Schreibstils**, die ich vorher noch klären möchte. Ich bin mir immer noch ein bisschen unsicher, wie man **einen Brief** im Englischen **beendet** - es scheint so viele verschiedene Arten zu geben, einen Brief abzuschließen ... .

Do's and Don'ts - A matter of form ...

When writing a **formal business letter**, the correct form of address is: **Dear Sir** or **Dear Madam.** The customary plural form is: **Dear Sirs/Mesdames.**
If you are writing a business letter **to a person you know by name** then you may now begin your letter in the following way:
Dear Mr (Smith, Brown). Difficulty is encountered by the British (and Americans) when a woman is addressed. If you are replying to a letter written by a woman who gave her name as Mrs then you can safely address her as: **Dear Mrs (Smith, Brown)**. A big problem arises when you have to reply to a letter signed **simply with surname and first name** - Joan Brown, for instance. Under no circumstances can you address her as Miss Brown. In the United States, the problem was

solved by inventing a new form - **Ms** - and this has also won wide acceptance now in Britain. So, replying to a letter signed by Joan Brown, you can safely address her as **Ms Brown**. Another alternative in use is to address her as: **Dear Joan Brown.**

Titles must always be used: Dear Lord Salisbury, Dear Sir John (here the surname is dropped!), **Dear Dr. Linklater, Dear Professor Maugham.**
Senior military ranks are also usually used in formal letter-writing: **Dear Major Rigby**.

And now - **how do you end a letter**?
Yours sincerely or **Yours faithfully**? The British use a simple rule in deciding whether to end a business letter with **»sincerely«** or **»faithfully«**. If the letter begins with a **»Dear Sir«** they avoid employing a further »S« by ending the letter **»Yours faithfully«**. The same rule applies if the letter begins **»Dear Madam«** or **»Dear Sirs/Mesdames«**.
»Yours sincerely« is reserved for letters addressed to persons by name: »Dear Mr Smith, Dear Mrs Brown etc.«. The form **»Yours truly«** is now found almost exclusively on letters sent by fax or electronic mail. The British have an almost limitless list of ways of ending letters addressed to persons by their first name: **Dear John ... with best wishes, with kind regards, with regards, all the best ...**

Train Yourself

Wie würden Sie die folgenden Briefe beenden?

1. Dear Major Trowbridge, I hope you got home safely after the wedding ...
2. Dear Sirs/Mesdames, We are writing to request ...
3. Dear James, Thank you for your invitation to dinner ...
4. Dear Sir Charles, My society would like to invite you to address ...
5. Dear Mr Spencer, We would like to place an order with your company for ...
6. Dear Mary, How pleased we were to hear your marvellous news ...
7. Dear Sir, We are writing to remind you that payment of the following account is due ...
8. Dear Lord Portbury, It would be a great honour for us if you were able to attend our open day ...

Talk Talk Talk

(Peter's Office. Melissa, the Marketing-Manager, enters)

(Peters Büro. Melissa, die Marketing-Managerin, tritt ein)

M. Good morning Peter, you look busy.

M. Guten Morgen Peter, Sie sehen beschäftigt aus.

P. I have this **pile of letters to attend to**. They'll take a lot of **getting through**.

P. Ich muss diesen **Haufen Briefe bearbeiten**. Es wird eine Weile dauern, bis ich sie **durch habe**.

M. If you need any help or advice, give me a call – particularly if they concern marketing, of course.

M. Rufen Sie mich an, falls Sie Hilfe oder einen Rat brauchen – besonders, wenn es um Marketing-Fragen geht, versteht sich.

P. That's very kind of you, Melissa. But I must try first of all to master these things myself.

P. Das ist sehr nett von Ihnen, Melissa, aber ich sollte vor allem versuchen, solche Aufgaben selbst zu bewältigen.

Peter's first letter is a **formal request** from a large retail company for information about ERGO's range of products:

Dear Sirs/Mesdames,

We would be most grateful if you sent us **at your convenience** full information about the range of the software products you are able to offer. We are particularly interested in any product you have which could lead to a streamlining of our sales and receipts accounting and recording systems.
Looking forward to your reply,
Yours faithfully,

John Mitchell,
Managing Director,
The Rosings Group

Talk Talk Talk

(Peter's office)

P. Steve? Hello, how are you today? I have a request here for information on **our full range of products**, but with special interest in anything in the **retail trade** area. We do have a **sales and receipts accounting program**, don't we?

S. Yes, but we're not having a great deal of success with it. It's already a year old and, in computer terms, has long passed its **'sell-by' date.** But I'm expecting an updated system from America at any time. **Can you put them off**?

P. Well, they seem to be in some hurry. Can I at least send off the other information?

S. Sure, but if they're retail trade they won't be interested in most of our other programmes. But I'll let you have the lot. I'll tell you what – I'll do more. I have a new secretary. She'll help you **draft that letter** in such a way they'll wait till next

(Peters Büro)

P. Steve? Hallo, wie geht es Ihnen heute? Ich habe hier eine Anfrage nach Informationen über unsere gesamte **Produktpalette**, besonders über alles, was den Bereich **Einzelhandel** betrifft. Wir haben doch ein **Verkaufs- und Quittungs-Buchführungsprogramm**, oder?

S. Ja, aber wir haben keinen besonderen Erfolg damit. Es ist bereits ein Jahr alt und hat für Computer-Verhältnisse sein **Verfallsdatum** schon lange überschritten. Allerdings erwarte ich täglich ein aktualisiertes System aus Amerika. **Können Sie die Leute noch ein bisschen hinhalten**?

P. Tja, sie scheinen es recht eilig zu haben. Kann ich ihnen wenigstens die anderen Informationen schicken?

S. Klar, aber wenn sie im Einzelhandel tätig sind, werden sie sich für die meisten unserer anderen Programme nicht sonderlich interessieren. Ich werde Ihnen trotzdem den ganzen Schwung geben. Ich sage Ihnen was – ich tue noch mehr. Ich habe eine neue Sekre-

Christmas for the retail sales programme. Her name's Beryl ...

tärin. Sie wird Ihnen helfen, **diesen Brief so zu entwerfen**, dass die glatt bis Weihnachten auf das Einzelhandels-Programm warten. Ihr Name ist Beryl ...

Peter und Beryl machen sich an die Arbeit:

Dear Mr Mitchell,

Thank you for **your inquiry** of May 4. **We have great pleasure in enclosing** complete information on the full range of our products. You will, however, notice that one important product is missing: the ERGO retail sales and receipts logging and accounting program. This is because the program is being replaced by a revolutionary new software which will be reaching us from the United States shortly.
We would not want to interest you in a program which is so soon to be overtaken by the very latest technology, and we assure you that immediately we receive the new software we shall get again in touch with you and arrange to demonstrate the new development to you personally.
Assuring you of our best attention at all times,

Yours sincerely,

Peter Brückner,
Assistant Managing Director,
ERGO Limited

Background Information

The British use the American spelling for »programme« in context of computers »We want to install your **accounting program**.«

Train Yourself

Bestimmen Sie die Nomina der folgenden Verben nach diesem Beispiel:
I *instructed* him to send me the documents as soon as possible.
Lösung: *instruction*.

1. May I *request* a speedy reply? request
2. I would like to *ask* you the following question ... request
3. We are now forced to *demand* immediate payment of the outstanding account. demand
4. We have no alternative but to *refuse* payment until all the conditions have been met. refusal
5. Our marketing department has had to *reject* your proposal. rejection
6. There's no point in *denying* your responsibility in the following matter.
7. We have no choice but to *withhold* payment until the equipment is seen to perform correctly.
8. We are able to *offer* you the following terms: ...

Talk Talk Talk

P. Well, that should do the trick. Thank you very much, Beryl.

P. Okay, so dürfte es klappen. Vielen Dank, Beryl.

B. That's quite all right, Mr Brückner. Any time. I'll put the letter in the **out-tray for posting**, shall I?

B. Gern geschehen, Mr Brückner. Jederzeit. Ich werde den Brief jetzt in den **Postausgangs-Korb** legen, in Ordnung?

P. I think I'd better show it to Mr Morgan first.

P. Ich glaube, ich zeige ihn besser zuerst Mr Morgan.

B. Just as you wish. The letter is **stored** anyway. I created a **new file** for the Rosings Group. You'll find it there.

B. Wie Sie wollen. Der Brief ist auf alle Fälle **abgespeichert**. Ich habe eine **neue Datei** für die Rosings Group angelegt. Da finden Sie ihn.

P. Well, I hope there'll be more to go in that file later on. Now for the next letter – oh dear, this one's a **complaint**.

P. Gut, ich hoffe, dieser Ordner wird später noch um einiges dicker werden. Jetzt aber zum nächsten Brief – oh weia, eine **Beschwerde**.

Dear Sirs/Mesdames,

I regret to have to inform you that my company is **not** at all **pleased with** the way in which the servicing contract for the ERGO office-management system is being honoured. According to the contract, an ERGO representative should visit our offices in person once a month during the 12-month period after installation. Our system was installed seven months ago and your Newcastle representative, Mr Batty, has called on us personally just twice. He has phoned on occasion to check if the system is functioning satisfactorily. Fortunately, the system has given us no problems, but there are technical questions which we need to discuss on a one-to-one basis and not over the telephone.
I would be pleased if you rectified the situation and honoured the terms of the contract.
Hoping to hear from you forthwith,

Yours faithfully,
George Robertson,
Managing Director,
The Newcastle Fine Produce Company

P. Lucy, I have a letter here to dictate, but first of all could you get me Mr Batty in Newcastle on the phone?

P. Lucy, ich habe hier einen Brief zum Diktieren, aber könnten Sie mich bitte zuerst mit Mr Batty in Newcastle verbinden?

L. Certainly, Peter.

L. Natürlich, Peter.

P. Hello, is that Desmond Batty? Peter Brückner of ERGO here. We've had a complaint from Newcastle Fine Foods that you

P. Hallo, spreche ich mit Desmond Batty? Hier spricht Peter Brückner von ERGO. Wir hatten hier eine Beschwerde der Newcastle Fine

haven't been following up that office-management systems installation as required in the contract.

Foods darüber, dass Sie ihr Büromanagement-System nicht betreut haben, wie es im Vertrag vereinbart ist.

D. I established that the system is working well and there was really no need to call by on a regular basis. George Robertson appeared to be in agreement.

D. Ich habe mich davon überzeugt, dass die Anlage einwandfrei funktioniert und dass es wirklich keinen Grund gibt, regelmäßig vorbeizukommen. George Robertson schien damit einverstanden zu sein.

P. Well, he's written us a pretty stiff letter of complaint. Can I tell him you'll be calling by as arranged monthly?

P. Tja, er hat uns einen ziemlich bestimmten Beschwerdebrief geschickt. Können Sie ihm mitteilen, dass Sie in Zukunft wie vereinbart monatlich vorbeischauen?

D. Well, if that's really what he wants, then fine by me. But there's actually nothing to do.

D. Gut, wenn er das unbedingt will, dann ist mir das recht. Aber es gibt dort wirklich nichts zu tun.

P. I think he just wants the reassurance that somebody from ERGO is **on the spot** and taking a personal interest in his **office management**.

P. Ich glaube er braucht lediglich die Gewissheit, dass jemand von ERGO **vor Ort** ist und persönliches Interesse an seinem **Büromanagement** zeigt.

D. Fine, then tell him I'll come round next Monday – and then once a month.

D. Gut, dann sagen Sie ihm, dass ich Montag bei ihm vorbeikomme – und danach einmal im Monat.

Dear Mr Robertson,

I am truly sorry you have had cause to complain about the way ERGO is honouring its contract with your company. There appears to have been a misunderstanding here. Mr Batty has not been calling personally as arranged because the system has been performing satisfactorily.

He most certainly would have visited your offices immediately if his help had been required.
I talked to Mr Batty by phone today and he promised to call personally next Monday and then once a month, as contractually arranged.
Assuring you of our best attention at all times,

Yours sincerely,
Peter Brückner

Train Yourself

Welche Wörter passen in die Lücken?

Dear Sir,
We would be very ________ if you ________ us information about your company's full ________ of ________.
We are interested in various ________ which have been ________ by your company, and we are sure we could ________ them in various ________ of our ________.
We have a board meeting ________ for next Wednesday, so it would be particularly ________ if you could ________ to send the information material to us by then.
Looking forward to your ________
Yours ________

scheduled, faithfully, range, sent, reply, developed, areas, useful, operations, arrange, products, employ, grateful.

Talk Talk Talk

(Steve enters Peter's office)

(Steve betritt Peters Büro)

S. Still **submerged in letters**? It's nearly lunch-time – I feel like a beer and a steak-pie at the *Duke of Rutland*. Want to join me?

S. Immer noch **unter einem Briefberg begraben**? Wir haben fast Mittag – ich hätte Lust auf ein Bier und eine Fleischpastete im *Duke of Rutland*. Möchten Sie mitkommen?

P. Oh, why not – I'll work late with the other letters if I have to.

P. Oh, warum nicht – ich werde wegen der restlichen Briefe eben länger arbeiten, wenn es nötig ist.

B. Wait for me then, I've **worked up a thirst** myself.

B. Warten Sie auf mich, ich bin **vom Arbeiten ganz durstig** geworden.

S. **Make it snappy** then, Beryl ...

S. Dann **machen Sie schnell**, Beryl ...

(The *Duke of Rutland* pub)
S. What's it to be, Peter, the usual?

(Im *Duke of Rutland*-Pub)
S. Was darf's denn sein Peter, das Übliche?

P. Yes please, Steve.

P. Ja bitte, Steve.

S. And Beryl?

S. Und Beryl?

B. An alcohol-free, please, Steve. Writing letters in English must be quite different from how you compose letters in German, Peter?

B. Bitte ein Alkoholfreies, Steve. Briefe auf Englisch zu schreiben ist sicher etwas ganz anderes, als das in Deutsch zu tun, oder, Peter?

P. There are small points of difference, but the general style is very similar. I had expected much less **formality** in English, but the rules are really just as rigid as in German.

P. Es gibt ein paar kleine Unterschiede, aber der generelle Stil ist ganz ähnlich. Ich hatte im Englischen viel weniger **Förmlichkeit** erwartet, aber die Regeln sind tatsächlich ebenso streng wie im Deutschen.

S. You're right there about formality and rules. But they're really only a cover, you know – I'll give you an example. Look at this letter I got this morning from my local council ...

S. Sie haben Recht, was die Formalitäten und Regeln angeht. Aber sie sind lediglich eine oberflächliche Hülle – ich werde es Ihnen demonstrieren. Schauen Sie sich diesen Brief an, den ich heute Morgen von meiner Stadtverwaltung bekommen habe ...

Dear Sir,

It has been brought to our attention that you are parking your car illegally on council land at the end of Lansdowne Drive, Wimbledon. Although the land has not yet been fenced off there are two notices making it very clear that parking is prohibited. You have been observed on several occasions parking your car on this ground at night and driving your vehicle away the next morning before our parking wardens take up their duty. For security reasons, even night-time parking is prohibited. Hence, **we must ask you kindly to refrain from** parking your car on this terrain in the future. Failure to comply with our request will result in legal action having to be taken against you.

Yours faithfully,

Edmond Tracey,
Town Clerk

Train Yourself

Finden Sie einfachere Wörter oder Ausdrücke für folgende:

1. prohibited ....
2. observed .... Seen
3. on several occasions .... severel times
4. take up their duty .... Start work
5. refrain from .... Stop
6. terrain .... Land

Talk Talk Talk

B. So why are you getting so **het-up**, Steve? It looks like an **open-and-shut** case to me.

B. Warum **regen** *Sie sich so* **auf**, Steve? Für mich sieht das wie ein **ganz klarer** Fall aus.

S. No. That's not it. Look at the style of that letter. They're basically telling me: »Hey, you **berk**, stop parking your **lousy** car on our ground«. But this guy Tracey has wrapped the brick up in fancy paper.

S. Nein, darum geht es nicht. Sehen Sie sich den Stil an, in dem dieser Brief geschrieben wurde. Was sie mir eigentlich sagen, ist: »He du **Dussel**, hör endlich auf, dein **lausiges** Auto auf unserem Grundstück zu parken.«
Aber dieser Tracey hat den Pflasterstein in Geschenkpapier verpackt.

B. Oh, come on, Steve. He's just being polite.

B. Ach, kommen Sie, Steve. Er ist doch nur höflich.

S. Yes, in that typically English way where it means **zilch.**

S. Ja, aber eben auf diese typisch englische Art und Weise, die ungefähr **gar nichts** bedeutet.

P. Well, I don't want to take sides here, but official letters like that are also **couched** in polite terms in Germany.

P. Na ja, ich möchte hier zwar keine Partei ergreifen, aber offizielle Briefe wie dieser sind in Deutschland auch in höfliche Formulierungen **eingebettet**.

Train Yourself

1. Beryl kann Steve zu einem freundlichen Antwortbrief überreden.
Können Sie die Lücken darin füllen?

Dear Mr Tracey,

Thank you for your letter of June 4. I am sorry you have had cause to inform me that I have been illegally parking on council land. In my defence, I must say that I was unaware that the land in question belonged to the council. I certainly saw no notices prohibiting parking. I had assumed that at night at least the land could be used to park cars on. If this is not the case, I shall of course ________ from parking my

car there in future. But may I take this opportunity to appeal for more car-parking possibilities in Lansdowne Drive and the vicinity.
Yours sincerely,

Steve Blackman

vicinity, opportunity, in question, cause, appeal, refrain, inform, used, unaware, prohibiting, assumed, defence.

2. In Großbritannien gibt es verschiedene Möglichkeiten zum Versenden eines Briefes. **Wie kann man diese am besten umschreiben?**

Registered post

(a) The recipient signs for the letter.
(b) The sender receives a receipt confirming the letter has seen sent.
(c) A description of the letter's contents is officially registered.

Recorded delivery

(a) The sender must sign a declaration assuming responsibility for the letter's delivery.
(b) The Post Office takes responsibility for the safe delivery of the letter.
(c) The recipient signs an official receipt confirming acceptance of the letter.

Background Information

And don't forget to stamp your letters - but with which stamps? Letters are sent by two alternative routes:
a. First Class - guaranteeing next-day delivery.
b. Second Class - where delivery can take two or three days.

Talk Talk Talk

(James Morgan enters Peter's office)
J. Peter, I have a letter here I'd like you to reply to today, if you can. It's a **job inquiry** which has

(James Morgan tritt in Peters Büro ein)
J. Peter, ich habe hier einen Brief, den Sie bitte noch heute beantworten sollten, wenn es Ihnen

been hidden among my **papers** for the past few days.

möglich ist. Es ist eine **Bewerbung**, die ein paar Tage lang unter meinen **Unterlagen** versteckt lag.

P. Certainly, Mr Morgan. But how should I reply to it?

P. Natürlich, Mr Morgan. Aber wie soll ich darauf antworten?

J. Just say we have no immediate vacancies but that we'll **put the application on file**. The young man certainly has qualifications which we might be able to use some time in the future. Just dictate the letter to Lucy.

J. Sagen Sie einfach, dass wir derzeit keine freien Stellen haben, **das Stellengesuch** jedoch **in die Datei aufnehmen**. Der junge Mann hat offensichtlich Qualifikationen, die uns in Zukunft vielleicht einmal nützlich sein könnten. Diktieren Sie den Brief einfach Lucy.

P. May I see the application?

P. Darf ich die Bewerbung mal sehen?

Dear Sir/Madam,

I am writing to inquire if your company has **an opening for a trainee in business management**. I have just completed my Master's degree in Business Administration at the University of Aston and am looking for an opportunity to add practical experience now to the theoretical knowledge I built up in five years of study. Your company was recommended to me by the University's professional counselling service. I am attaching a brief **CV** which summarizes my educational background.

Yours faithfully,

Martin Russell

P. Lucy, could you **take a letter** please?

P. Lucy, können Sie bitte einen **Brief aufnehmen**?

L. Certainly, Peter ...

L. Natürlich, Peter ...

Dear Mr Russell,

Thank you for your letter of May 22. **We regret to inform you** that at the moment we have no vacancy which would suit your qualifications. But we would be most interested in meeting you if such a vacancy occurred in the future and we shall be glad to put your inquiry in our files. **In the meantime**, please accept an up-to-date information brochure on ERGO Limited.

Yours sincerely,

Peter Brückner,
Assistant Managing Director

Train Yourself

Der folgende Beschwerdebrief landet auf Peters Schreibtisch:

Dear Sir,

Your sales representative in Birmingham promised one month ago to call by our offices and explain the advantages of the ERGO Accounting 2000 package. We suspended inquiries we had begun with other companies pending the outcome of the meeting with your representative. To this date, no ERGO representative has reported to us. I **regret** to have to inform you that our Board has decided that unless we hear from your representative within one week of the date of this letter we shall be compelled to **strike** ERGO **from** our short-list of possible suppliers and look elsewhere for the product we urgently need.

Yours faithfully,

Eric Simpson,
Director,
Titan Products

Helfen Sie Peter dabei, James Morgan vom Inhalt des Briefes zu unterrichten, indem Sie die richtige Form der Verben in den Klammern benutzen!

Mr Simpson of Titan Products *(write)* to us *(complain)* that although our sales representative in Birmingham *(promise)* to call by his offices (*explain*) our Accounting 2000 system he *(not turn up)*. Mr Simpson *(tell)* us that Titan *(suspend)* inquiries with other possible suppliers until the company *(look at)* our product. He *(say)* the Titan Board *(decide ... give)* us one more week for our representative *(call)*. If he *(not do so)* within that time Titan *(strike)* us from its short-list of possible suppliers and *(look)* elsewhere for a supplier.

Talk Talk Talk

(Melissa enters Peter's office)

(Melissa betritt Peters Büro)

M. How are you getting along, Peter, in your search for a place to live?

M. Wie kommen Sie bei Ihrer Suche nach einer festen Bleibe voran, Peter?

P. Two agents are now looking for me, but frankly I just get more confused with each letter I receive from them.

P. Ich habe jetzt zwei Makler, die für mich auf der Suche sind, aber ehrlich gesagt verwirrt mich jeder Brief mehr, den ich von ihnen bekomme.

M. What's wrong with them?

M. Was stimmt denn damit nicht?

P. Well, maybe I'm a bit too demanding but whenever they send me descriptions of property I might be interested in and I arrange for a viewing I never find what I expect. Here's the latest example ...

P. Tja, vielleicht verlange ich einfach zuviel, aber jedes Mal, wenn sie mir Beschreibungen von Wohnungen schicken, die mich eventuell interessieren könnten und ich einen Besichtigungstermin vereinbare, finde ich nicht das vor, was ich erwarte. Hier das jüngste Beispiel ...

Dear Mr Brückner,

We are very pleased to be able to offer you a **highly desirable** property in one of the areas which you indicated to us might be of most interest to you as a **permanent location** to live. The property is on the first floor of a magnificently converted Victorian-era mansion. It **boasts** a representative entrance hall, two **generously-proportioned** bedrooms, a stately living room with separate dining area, Adam fireplace and corniced, built-in book-shelves, a spacious kitchen with every possible modern appliance, a luxurious bathroom with jacuzzi, substantial brass fittings and pastel-toned suite. Panoramic views to Hyde Park.
We **urge** a very early viewing of this unique property and **would be pleased to arrange an appointment at your kind convenience**.

Yours sincerely,
...

Train Yourself

Schreiben Sie den obigen Brief neu, indem Sie folgende Wörter und Ausdrücke durch diejenigen aus der unteren Auswahlliste ersetzen:

1. highly desirable ....
2. permanent location ....
3. boasts ....
4. generously-proportioned ....
5. urge ....

wanted, ask, recommend, luxurious, large, site, has, possesses, extensive, needed, attractive.

Talk Talk Talk

M. Well? Looks quite a place!

M. Und? Hört sich doch gut an!

P. Doesn't it just? There were even a couple of photographs with the letter. Here ...

P. Nicht wahr? Dem Brief waren sogar einige Fotos beigefügt. Hier ...

M. Wow! Now that's something ...

M. Donnerwetter! Das macht schon was her ...

P. The photographer who took them must have been quite something, too. They're not at all like what I saw with my own eyes!

P. Der Fotograf, der sie gemacht hat, muss auch ganz schön was her gemacht haben. Sie sehen nicht im geringsten so aus wie das, was ich mit meinen eigenen Augen gesehen habe!

M. You viewed the place?

M. Sie haben sich die Wohnung angesehen?

P. Of course. Would you like *my* description of it?

P. Natürlich. Würden Sie gern *meine* Beschreibung davon hören?

M. I'm **dying to** hear it!

M. Ich **sterbe vor** Neugier!

P. Right! Let's start with the entrance hall. »Representative« was the description. What it represented was a small space behind the front door, not large enough to put a hall-stand. Neither of the »generously-proportioned« bedrooms was larger than 12 square metres. »Stately« living room? It was **in a bit of a state,** that I'll admit. The »separate dining area« just didn't exist. The »Adam« fireplace was a plaster **mock-up,** and the bookshelves were a do-it-yourself job. Modern kitchen appliances? They might have been complete if there had been a dishwasher and a microwave. The »luxurious« bathroom was a converted cupboard with no window.

P. In Ordnung! Beginnen wir mit der Eingangshalle. »Repräsentativ« lautete die Beschreibung. Was sie repräsentierte war ein kleiner Raum hinter der Eingangstüre, nicht einmal groß genug, um eine Garderobe hineinzustellen. Keines der »großzügig geschnittenen« Schlafzimmer war größer als zwölf Quadratmeter. Wohnzimmer in »prächtigem Zustand«? Es war **ein Zustand**, das muss ich zugeben. Der »separate Essbereich« existierte einfach gar nicht. Der steinerne Kamin war eine **Nachbildung** aus Gips und die Bücherborde waren selbst gemacht. Moderne Kücheneinrichtung? Sie wären vielleicht komplett gewesen, wenn es eine Geschirrspülmaschine und eine

And so on. Want to hear more?

Mikrowelle gegeben hätte. Das »luxuriöse« Badezimmer war ein umgewandelter Schrank ohne Fenster. Und so weiter, und so fort. Wollen Sie noch mehr hören?

M. (laughs). No, that's enough, Peter. You've learnt another important lesson in Britain – never trust an estate agent's **hype.** Or learn how to read between the lines.

M. (lacht). Nein, das reicht, Peter. Sie haben eine weitere wichtige, englische Lektion gelernt – traue nie den **Übertreibungen** eines Wohnungsmaklers. Oder lerne, zwischen den Zeilen zu lesen.

P. Between the lines?

P. Zwischen den Zeilen?

M. Estate agents have their own language. If the bedrooms had been really large they would have been described as »huge« not »generously proportioned«, that kind of thing.

M. Wohnungsmakler haben ihre eigene Sprache. Wären die Schlafzimmer tatsächlich groß gewesen, wären sie als »riesig« und nicht als »großzügig geschnitten« beschrieben worden oder etwas in der Art.

P. Oh dear! I don't think I'll ever find a place to live.

P. Ach du meine Güte! Ich glaube, ich werde nie eine richtige Bleibe finden.

M. Patience, Peter, patience – a very English virtue!

M. Geduld, Peter, Geduld – eine englische Tugend!

Background Information

As Peter has now discovered, there are **various forms of English, employed in distinct situations and most visible in written letters**. A letter containing a very real threat of **dire** action will be written in as polite a form as the most harmless **missive**. But of all the various forms of English employed in official communications the most curious and most difficult to construe is the language used by estate agents in describing the properties they hope to sell. If you are renting or buying property in Britain through the services of an estate agent you would be well advised to engage the additional advice of somebody fluent in English.

Train Yourself

Setzen Sie die korrekte Form des Verbs »to write« ein!

1. I would ___ if I had only known your address.
2. I'll ___ just as soon as I arrive.
3. He ___ regularly won't he?
4. She has never ___ to me in that tone before.
5. I have better things to do than ___ to you all the time.
6. They ___ that they would be returning tomorrow.
7. I ___ to you right now, while waiting for the train.

Talk Talk Talk

P. Melissa, now here's a letter I really don't understand at all. It seems to belong in your department, but I'm not sure.

P. Melissa, ich habe hier einen Brief, den ich wirklich überhaupt nicht verstehe. Es scheint so, als würde er in Ihre Abteilung gehören, aber ich bin mir nicht sicher.

M. Let me take a look ...

M. Zeigen Sie mal ...

Dear Sirs/Mesdames,

Thank you for your letter of the 15th inst., **to which we now have pleasure in replying positively**. Your interest in participating in the joint InterConnect initiative has been noted and we have pleasure in enclos-

ing formal application forms. In view of the brief amount of time now remaining, may we urge you to forward us your application as soon as possible, together with the registration fee. The absolute deadline for applications is the 31st of July, and any applications received after that date can unfortunately not be accepted.
Looking forward to your reply,

Yours faithfully,
Robert Clarke

M. Oh dear, I don't know how that letter ended up on James's desk. I quite forgot that we had asked for information about participation in the Inter-Connect **marketing push**. I'll really have to get busy on this one – it's no wonder it had you puzzled, Peter.	M. Oh je, ich weiß nicht, wie dieser Brief auf James Tisch gelandet ist. Ich hatte fast vergessen, dass wir um Informationen über die Teilnahme an der InterConnect-**Marketinginitiative** gebeten hatten. Darum muss ich mich wirklich kümmern – kein Wunder, dass Sie verwirrt waren, Peter.
P. Well, there's one expression – or abbreviation there – that really **foxed** me, is that what you say? That *inst.* What does that mean?	P. Tja, es gibt da einen Ausdruck – oder Abkürzung – die mich wirklich **verblüfft** hat, ist das das richtige Wort? Dieses *inst.* Was bedeutet das?
M. Oh, that! It's just a formal way of referring to the month – in this case our letter was dated the 15th of July, or the 15th *inst.* The form is becoming obsolete, but you'll still meet it and it's good for you to know what it means.	M. Ach das! Das ist lediglich eine formelle Art und Weise, sich auf den jeweiligen Monat zu beziehen – in diesem Fall ist der Brief datiert auf den 15. Juli oder den 15. *inst.* Dieser Ausdruck ist langsam veraltet, aber er kommt manchmal noch vor und es ist gut, dass Sie jetzt wissen, was er bedeutet.
P. So today is the 21st *inst.*?	P. Also ist heute der 21. *inst.*?

M. Yes, but only in letter form – talking of which, do you have any more **to reply to**?

M. Ja, aber nur in schriftlicher Briefform – und da wir gerade davon sprechen, haben Sie noch welche **zu beantworten**?

P. Stacks – I'd better get down to them.

P. Haufenweise – ich kümmere mich besser darum.

M. Peter, a tip. Divide them up into categories. You'll save a lot of time that way. And then concentrate on those that have to be replied to urgently.

M. Peter, ein Tipp. Teilen Sie sie in Kategorien ein. So sparen Sie sich eine Menge Zeit. Und dann konzentrieren Sie sich auf diejenigen, die dringend beantwortet werden müssen.

P. Well, I suppose these **letters inquiring about** our products are the most pressing – I'll get down to those first ...

P. Tja, ich vermute, die **Briefe, in denen man sich nach** unseren Produkten **erkundigt**, sind die dringendsten – die werde ich zuerst bearbeiten ...

Train Yourself

Wählen Sie die richtigen Wörter um die Lücken zu füllen!

1. We have pleasure in acknowledging ________ of your letter.
2. Looking forward to a ________ reply.
3. We would ________ an ________ reply.
4. Please be ________ of our ________ attention at all times.
5. Would you please ________ to the above address.
6. We would be ________ if you ________ us information about your product-line.

reply, early, best, grateful, receipt, assured, appreciate, prompt, sent.

(Peter **tackles some letters of inquiry** ...)

(Peter **geht ein paar Anfragen durch** ...)

Dear Sir,

My attention was caught by your company's advertisement in Techno-News. **I am particularly interested in** the Reddy program, which your company claims can contribute to large savings of time in sorting bulk orders. Our growth in wholesale trade has now reached the point where a highly-developed technological system is needed to keep pace with increasing orders. I would, therefore, be most obliged if you arranged to send me further, detailed information on the Reddy program.

Yours faithfully,

Frank R. Gilpin,
Managing Director,
Top Trading

P. (reaches for his telephone) Steve, do you have the **information brochures** and **catalogues** on the Reddy program?

P. (greift nach dem Telefonhörer) Steve, haben Sie die **Informationsbroschüren und die Kataloge** über die Reddy-Programme?

S. Hang on a moment, I'll have a look. Yes, I've got a pile of stuff here.

S. Bleiben Sie einen Augenblick dran. Ich sehe nach. Ja, ich habe einen Stapel von dem Zeug hier.

P. I have an **inquiry** here for as much information as we can send. Brochures and catalogues. I'll give you a copy of my reply – you'll want to alert your man in Birmingham, there could be a sale here.

P. Ich habe hier eine **Anfrage** nach so viel Informationen, wie wir schicken können. Broschüren und Kataloge. Ich werde Ihnen eine Kopie meiner Antwort geben – Sie werden Ihren Mann in Birmingham sicher darauf aufmerksam machen wollen, dass hier ein Geschäft zustande kommen könnte.

S. Yes, **please keep me in touch**. It's good of you to take over this **correspondence**, dear chap. I have so much to do at the moment.

S. Ja, **halten Sie mich auf dem Laufenden**. Es ist nett von Ihnen, diesen **Schriftwechsel** zu übernehmen, alter Freund. Ich habe im Augenblick so viel zu tun.

P. No problem, Steve. It's a pleasure.

P. Kein Problem, Steve. Ist mir ein Vergnügen.

P. Lucy, can you **take a letter**?

P. Lucy, können Sie **einen Brief aufnehmen**?

L. Peter, you have a **dictaphone** in your desk, you know. Why don't you use that? It'll save us both time.

L. Peter, Sie haben ein **Diktiergerät** in Ihrer Schreibtischschublade. Warum benutzen Sie es nicht? Damit würden wir beide Zeit sparen.

P. Well, bless my soul, I should have known a high-tech company would have a device like that.

P. Meine Güte, ich hätte wissen sollen, dass ein Hightech-Unternehmen so einen Apparat haben würde.

P. Well, here goes...

P. Also, los geht's...

Reply to letter from Mr Frank Gilpin, Managing Director, Top Trading, Aston Road 20-14, Birmingham, dated the 14th of July.

Dear Mr Gilpin,

Thank you for your letter of July 14 (Lucy, make that 14th of July or 14.07., if you like, whatever our style is). **I have great pleasure in sending you full information** on the Reddy program which you requested. This is the **very latest development** in electronic order-sorting, and **we are sure it would match your requirements.**

If you have any further questions please do not hesitate to contact me. My telephone and telefax numbers are as above.

Yours sincerely,

Peter Brückner,
Assistant Managing Director,
ERGO Limited

P. Steve, how would you like a **copy** of this letter? A **hard copy** or shall I put it **on file**?

P. Steve, in welcher Form hätten Sie die **Kopie** dieses Briefes gerne? **Auf Papier** oder soll ich sie **in einer Datei** speichern?

S. Can you create a file for Top Trading and save it in that? You'll find a general file for business inquiries under »ERGO-Inquiries«. I have access to that and it keeps me up to date on possible **sales follow-ups**. I'm sure we'll be hearing more from Top Trading – at least, I hope we do.

S. Könnten Sie eine Datei für Top Trading erstellen und darin abspeichern? Unter »ERGO-Anfragen« finden Sie eine allgemeine Datei für Geschäftsanfragen. Ich habe Zugriff dazu und sie hält mich auf dem Laufenden über mögliche **Nachfolge-Verkäufe**. Ich bin mir sicher, wir werden noch mehr von Top Trading hören – wenigstens hoffe ich das.

Train Yourself

Peter findet es einfacher, seine Briefe mit Hilfe des Diktiergeräts an Lucy weiterzureichen. **Geben Sie in den folgenden Sätzen die korrekten Komparativformen an.**

1. This letter was much *(clear)* than the first one.
2. His last letter was *(brief)* than usual, but still *(long)* than hers.
3. Although it was written by hand, the letter was *(legible)* than I thought it would be.
4. The tone of that letter was *(insulting)* than I expected.
5. Why was the letter *(lengthy)* than the others.
6. The letter arrived *(soon)* than I had expected.

(Peter takes the next letter from the pile...)

(Peter nimmt den nächsten Brief vom Stapel)

Dear Mr Morgan,

I am taking the liberty of writing to you following our meeting at the Chamber of Trade lunch. I was very interested in your description of the range of activities of your company, and I would like to learn more. I would be most honoured if you accepted an invitation to lunch with me at my club next week. May I suggest Friday?
Looking forward to hearing from you,

Yours sincerely,

Henry Rowbotham

Talk Talk Talk

(Peter knocks at James Morgan's office and enters)

(Peter klopft an James Morgans Büro und tritt ein)

P. Mr Morgan, I believe this is a **personal letter** for you to answer. It was among the correspondence you gave me to attend to.

P. Mr Morgan, ich glaube dies ist ein **persönlicher Brief**, den Sie beantworten sollten. Er lag unter der Korrespondenz, die Sie mir zur Bearbeitung gegeben hatten.

J. Oh, Peter, I wanted to talk to you about that. I can't face a meeting with that man Rowbotham. He has really absolutely no interest in ERGO – I think he's just looking for a drinking partner. Could you reply for me, telling him I am **indisposed** for the next couple of weeks.

J. Oh Peter, darüber wollte ich mit Ihnen sprechen. Ich möchte mich auf keinen Fall mit diesem Rowbotham treffen. Er hat absolut kein Interesse an ERGO – ich glaube, er sucht nur jemanden, der mit ihm einen trinken geht. Könnten Sie für mich antworten und ihm mitteilen, dass ich die nächsten paar Wochen **unabkömmlich** bin?

P. I'll try, but I'd like to show you the letter before I send it ...

P. Ich werde es versuchen, aber ich würde Ihnen den Brief gerne zeigen, bevor ich ihn wegschicke.

Dear Mr Rowbotham,

Mr Morgan has asked me to reply to your letter and to your kind invitation to lunch. He is unable to do so himself because he is **unfortunately indisposed**. He much appreciates the interest you showed in the work of ERGO Limited, and he has asked me to forward to you all our available information on the activities of the company. **If you have further questions** on the company, **I shall be happy to answer** them for you.
Mr Morgan joins me in sending greetings,

Yours sincerely,

Peter Brückner,
Assistant Managing Director,
ERGO Limited

Talk Talk Talk

J. **That'll do very well**, Peter. Thank you. But you might have opened yourself to an invitation to lunch with Rowbotham ...

J. **Sehr gut gemacht**, Peter. Allerdings könnten Sie sich jetzt selbst der Gefahr einer Einladung zum Mittagessen von Mr Rowbotham ausgesetzt haben ...

P. I think **I can handle that**, Mr Morgan. Don't worry. That was a comparatively easy one – let's see what's next in the pile ...

P. Ich denke, **damit komme ich klar**, Mr Morgan. Keine Sorge. Das war ein vergleichsweise einfacher Brief – mal sehen, was das Nächste auf dem Stapel ist ...

Train Yourself

Sie sind zum Essen mit dem Managing Direktor einer großen Firma, Mr Gerald Green, eingeladen. Nachdem Sie zuerst angenommen haben, stellen Sie fest, dass Sie an dem Tag auf Geschäftsreise außerhalb der Stadt müssen.

Wie würden Sie dementsprechend eine angemessene Absage formulieren?

....

....

....

Vocabulary

berk	Dussel/Idiot (umgangssprachlich)
boast	prahlen (hier: etwas vorweisen können)
catch up on letter-writing	überfälligen Brief schreiben
complaint couch	Beschwerde formulieren, »sprachlich einbetten«
dire	gräßlich/ hier: weitreichend, unangenehm
to draft	entwerfen
dying to	»sterben« etwas zu sehen/ hören etc.
to end a letter	einen Brief beenden
fine by me	ist mir recht
foxed	verblüfft
generously-proportioned	großzügig geschnitten
to get through	durchkriegen
het-up	aufgeregt/erhitzt über etwas
highly desirable	höchst attraktiv
hype	zielgerichtete Übertreibung/»Hype«

in a state	hier: in einem schlechten Zustand
indisposed	unpässlich, auch unabkömmlich
inquiry	Anfrage
to inquire about	sich erkundigen nach
in the meantime	in der Zwischenzeit
in-tray	(Post-) Eingangskorb
lousy	lausig, verflixt
Make it snappy!	Machen Sie schnell/fix!
marketing push	Marketing-Initiative
missive	Mitteilung
on occasion	bei Gelegenheit
on the spot	vor Ort
open-and-shut	klar und deutlich/ eindeutig
out-tray	(Post-)Ausgangskorb
permanent location	ständiger Wohnsitz
push	Initiative/ Vorstoß (besonders im Marketing)
refrain from	sich zurückhalten
to reply to	beantworten
»sell-by« date	Haltbarkeitsdatum
stacks	Stapel (hier: »stapelweise«)
strike from	ausstreichen/herausnehmen
streamlining	Leistungssteigerung
to tackle some letters	ein paar Briefe durchgehen
to type up	abtippen
urge	inständig bitten, drängen
work up a thirst	»sich durstig arbeiten«
writer's cramp	Schreibkrampf
zilch	Nichts (umgangssprachlich)

Recommendations and complaints
Empfehlungen und Reklamationen

Here we go

Nachdem Peter jede Menge Briefverkehr für seinen Vorgesetzten zu erledigen hatte, konnte er sich schnell auf diesem Gebiet einarbeiten. Aber er muss nun leider der Tatsache ins Auge sehen, dass bei der Korrespondenz die Beschwerdebriefe eine wichtige Rolle spielen und dass der Anlass zu diesen Beschwerden schnellstmöglich aus der Welt geschafft werden muss ...

Talk Talk Talk

(Peter's office)	(Peters Büro)
P. Well, it's good to find complimentary letters as well as complaints ...	P. Tja, es ist ja schön, neben Beschwerdebriefen auch einmal lobende Post zu bekommen ...

Dear Sirs, Mesdames,

We are writing to compliment your company on the performance of your software package Accounting 2000 and the efficiency of the post-sales servicing. We first became aware of the program through the recommendation of Philips and Company, who also are highly pleased with the product. At a time when we were considering **subcontracting** a section of our accounting work, the program cut our work-load by a full thirty per cent and our two accountants are now able easily to **keep abreast** with the demands placed on them by our growing business. They are particularly happy with the **user-friendly** nature of the software and had no difficulty adjusting traditional accounting practices to the new technology.
Like you, we have great faith in the future of this new technology and would like to contribute to its progress. As a satisfied ERGO customer,

we can do much to **propagate** Accounting 2000 and would be happy to do so. An appropriate commission on orders completed as a result of our recommendation would be a material encouragement, and may we suggest a meeting to discuss a suitable arrangement of mutual benefit? Our Managing Director, Mr John Prestwick, can make himself available at any time during the next three weeks for such a meeting, which we believe could result in **considerable** advantages for both companies.

Yours faithfully,

Toby Samuels,
Company Secretary **(signing on behalf of Mr Prestwick)**

P. Hmm. This appears to be a problem letter as well as a complimentary one ...

P. Hmm. Das scheint ein ebenso problematischer wie schmeichelhafter Brief zu sein ...

(James Morgan's office)

(James Morgans Büro)

P. Good morning, Mr Morgan. I have a letter here which I'm not sure how to respond to.

P. Guten Morgen, Mr Morgan. Ich habe hier einen Brief, bei dem ich mir nicht sicher bin, wie ich darauf antworten soll.

J. Let me see. Hmm, looks like a not-too-**subtle** attempt to make money out of us, doesn't it?

J. Lassen Sie mal sehen. Hmm, sieht aus wie ein nicht besonders **subtiler** Versuch, Geld aus uns rauszukitzeln, stimmt's?

P. It does rather. But it puts us in a difficult position, don't you think?

P. Ja, so ziemlich. Aber er bringt uns auch in eine **schwierige Lage**, meinen Sie nicht auch?

J. How do you mean?

J. Wie meinen Sie das?

P. Well, if we refuse, Samuels or Prestwick could theoretically cause **problems** for us. I mean, it would

P. Nun ja, wenn wir uns weigern, könnten Samuels oder Prestwick uns theoretisch Ärger machen. Ich

be as easy to **rubbish** Accounting 2000 as to recommend it further, wouldn't it?

meine, es wäre genauso einfach, Accounting 2000 **mies** zu **machen**, wie es weiter zu empfehlen.

J. Rubbish? Your English vocabulary is widening by the day.

J. Mies zu machen? Ihr Wortschatz wird von Tag zu Tag größer.

P. I have to thank Steve for that!

P. Das verdanke ich Steve!

J. Perhaps Steve has a useful contribution to make here – I do agree with you that a suitable reply to the letter does pose problems.

J. Vielleicht kann Steve hier etwas Nützliches beisteuern – ich stimme mit Ihnen überein, dass eine passende Antwort auf den Brief Probleme aufwirft.

P. I'll show the letter to Steve, then, and report back ...

P. Dann zeige ich Steve den Brief und melde mich wieder ...

Background Information

A matter of words ...

Slang has long crept into business English usage and even into formal business letters. The noun »rubbish« (Müll, Abfall) has given rise to a slang verb, to rubbish, meaning to talk badly about. It's another example of the flexibility of the English language, which accommodates quite easily the movement of words from one category to another (here from noun to verb).

Train Yourself

Die folgenden Sätze sind einem Geschäftsbrief entnommen. **Suchen Sie die Wörter aus, die am besten passen.**

1. I would like to __________ your company on the __________ of its post-sales servicing.

a. recommend
b. praise
c. commend

a. promise
b. efficiency
c. efficacy

2. Please be ________ enough as to send us information material as ________ as possible.

a. gracious
b. generous
c. good

a. promptly
b. timely
c. rapidly

3. We have the ________ duty to ________ you that the delivery was not only late but incomplete.

a. unfortunate
b. unhappy
c. unpleasant

a. tell
b. inform
c. remind

4. Unless we ________ satisfaction in this matter we shall be ________ to instruct our lawyers to take action.

a. get
b. find
c. obtain

a. compelled
b. forced
c. obliged

Talk Talk Talk

P. Hi Steve, did you read that letter? Do you have any ideas on how to reply to it?	P. Hallo Steve, haben Sie den Brief gelesen? Haben Sie irgend eine Idee, wie man darauf antworten soll?
S. Sure.	S. Sicher.
P. And?	P. Ja und?
S. Well, my first idea is **to junk** it.	S. Na ja, meine erste Idee war, ihn **wegzuschmeißen**.
P. Junk?	P. Wegzuschmeißen?

S. **Bin** it, crumple it up and **chuck** it in the waste-basket.

S. **Wirf** ihn **weg**, knüll ihn zusammen und **schmeiß** ihn in den Mülleimer.

P. No, come on – joking aside, I have to reply to it on Morgan's behalf.

P. Ach nein, kommen Sie schon – Spaß beiseite, ich muss ihn in Morgans Auftrag beantworten.

S. OK, I've drafted something that might **do the trick** ...

S. In Ordnung, ich habe da was ausgetüftelt, das **funktionieren könnte** ...

Dear Mr Samuels,

Thank you very much for your letter of May 14. We at ERGO Limited **were delighted to hear of your satisfaction** with the accounting program 2000, and we appreciate very much that you took the trouble to write us such a letter of commendation.
Your proposal of commissions on contracts arising from your recommendation is basically acceptable to us, but **we must ask you to elaborate in more detail on what you have in mind**. Our commission policy and structure – in line with most other companies – is fairly complicated. For instance, we distinguish between recommendations and **referrals** which result in signed contracts. Furthermore, the commission structure is affected by the role of our salesmen in following up so-called leads. We would be happy to hear your ideas on this subject and would then be very pleased to take part in a meeting to discuss a further course of action.

Yours faithfully,

Peter Brückner,
Assistant Managing Director

P. So how does that letter solve the problem, Steve?

P. Und wie soll dieser Brief jetzt unser Problem lösen, Steve?

S. In two ways. First, we **blind** them **with science** – I'm sure they have never before had to distinguish between recommendations and referrals. And then we play the ball straight back into their court. I'd be surprised if we heard anything more.

S. In doppelter Hinsicht. Als erstes **verwirren** wir sie mit **Fachbegriffen** – ich bin mir sicher, sie mussten noch niemals zuvor zwischen Empfehlungen und Vermittlungen unterscheiden. Und dann spielen wir den Ball noch direkt zurück in ihr Spielfeld. Es würde mich wundern, wenn wir von denen noch mal irgend etwas hören würden.

P. But couldn't their proposal actually have won us more business?

P. Aber hätte uns ihre Anfrage nicht ein weiteres Geschäft eingebracht?

S. Perhaps, but it would also have brought problems. The Accounting 2000 system is so successful **it sells itself. Personal recommendations** help, and they'll come anyway. But when you get into the **grey zone** of **direct referrals** which result in contracts you find yourself in tricky territory – ask any of our sales personnel.

S. Vielleicht, aber es hätte uns auch Probleme eingehandelt. Das Accounting 2000-System ist so erfolgreich, dass **es sich** quasi **von selbst verkauft. Persönliche Empfehlungen** sind hilfreich und kommen so oder so. Aber wenn man in die **Grauzone direkter Vermittlungen** gerät, die auf Verträge hinauslaufen, gerät man auf unsicheren Boden – da konnen Sie jeden der Mitarbeiter aus dem Verkauf fragen.

False Friends

Don't confuse **personal** and **personnel**!
»Personal« is an adjective, which has the general meaning of private, individual, peculiar or proper to a person. »Personnel« is a noun, meaning a group of employees in an enterprise. There is also a difference in pronounciation (pérsonal/personnél).

Recommendation and referral ...

If something is recommended its qualities are praised. The praise is a recommendation: »This is the best brand of tea I've found yet – I really do recommend it.«

If something is referred, attention is drawn to it – the act of referring becomes a referral, a common sales expression. »I gave their sales staff several names of companies who had expressed interest in the products on offer – I couldn't have given them a better list of referrals.«

Train Yourself

»Personal« oder »personnel«? »Recommendation« oder »referral«? **Wie lautet der richtige Begriff?**

1. I told him I wanted to speak to him on a _____ matter, affecting only him and me.
2. After assessing the _____ performances of various staff members I told the General Manager I had to speak to him on a _____ matter.
3. The company is interested only in how employees perform at their job. _____ problems never find their way into our _____ files.
4. On the strength of the _____ from this most important client, we asked the Head of Sales to establish contact with the company.
5. Our sales representative in Newcastle has passed on several _____, which we shall be following up.
6. We thought it was a promising _____ but when we called there appeared to be no interest.

Talk Talk Talk

(Peter's Office)	(Peters Büro)
M. Good morning, Peter. How's the letter-writing?	M. Guten Morgen, Peter. Wie klappt es mit dem Briefe schreiben?
P. Hello, Melissa. It's like **painting the Forth Bridge**. I thought yester-	P. Hallo Melissa. Ungefähr so, als müsste ich **die Forth Bridge**

day I'd got the upper hand of the job, and now I've got this pile of **freshly-arrived correspondence** to tackle.

anmalen (etwas schier Unmögliches schaffen). Gestern dachte ich noch, ich hätte die Oberhand über den Job gewonnen und jetzt habe ich diesen Stapel **frisch hereingekommener Briefe** zu bewältigen.

M. Eventually, we'll need an assistant to the Assistant General Manager. Can't James help?

M. Am Ende werden wir noch einen Assistenten des Assistenten des leitenden Direktors brauchen. Kann Ihnen James nicht helfen?

P. **He's off this week** at a managerial symposium. I know he feels uncomfortable about leaving me with this work-load. Not to worry, I'll get through it.

P. **Er ist diese Woche außer Haus** auf einem Manager-Symposium. Ich weiß, ihm ist nicht wohl dabei, mich mit so einer Ladung Arbeit allein zu lassen. Aber keine Bange, ich werde schon damit fertig.

M. Look, if you really do need any help let me know and I'll **assign** you Beryl again.

M. Passen Sie auf, falls Sie doch noch Hilfe brauchen, sagen Sie Bescheid und ich **teile** Ihnen Beryl noch einmal **zu**.

P. Thanks, Melissa, but I think I'll manage. You gave me some good advice when you said I should divide the correspondence into categories. The only problem is the biggest category seems to be letters of complaint. I had one warm letter of recommendation yesterday, but today the post brought a couple of real **stinkers**. Look at this one ...

P. Danke Melissa, aber ich glaube ich kriege das hin. Sie haben mir wirklich einen guten Rat gegeben, als Sie sagten, ich solle die Korrespondenz in Kategorien aufteilen. Das einzige Problem dabei ist, dass die umfangreichste Kategorie die der Beschwerdebriefe zu sein scheint. Gestern hatte ich noch einen netten Brief mit Empfehlungen dabei, aber heute hat mir die Post ein paar richtig **harte Brocken** gebracht. Schauen Sie sich mal den hier an...

Sirs!

More than one month has now passed since we requested you to send us complete information about your AGIT software program. To date, nothing at all has arrived, and unless we hear forthwith from you with complete documentation – i.e. information brochures and catalogues – we shall be compelled to turn elsewhere. We would regret having to do this, particularly in view of the recommendation we have received from two sources who are highly satisfied with the program. Hoping to hear from you without further delay,

We remain, Sirs,

Yours sincerely,

Severn and Sons,
Worcester

M. Looks like one for Steve.	M. Sieht nach einem Fall für Steve aus.
P. I think you're right. Something seems to have gone really wrong in the Sales Department.	P. Ich glaube, Sie haben Recht. Da scheint im Verkauf etwas richtig schief gegangen zu sein.
M. Why don't you call him in – you're theoretically the boss now James is **off base**. Come on, show us what you are made of!	M. Warum rufen Sie ihn nicht an – theoretisch sind Sie der Chef, jetzt wo James **nicht da** ist. Kommen Sie schon – zeigen Sie uns jetzt, woraus Sie geschnitzt sind!
P. Well, not with you around, Melissa.	P. Na ja, nicht so lange Sie hier sind, Melissa.
M. OK, but I'd like to know the outcome of this one.	M. In Ordnung, aber ich möchte wissen, was dabei rauskommt.

P. I'll keep you informed – as they seem to say all the time in this business ...
(reaches for the phone) Hi, Steve, can I have a word with you?

P. Ich halte Sie auf dem Laufenden – wie man in diesem Geschäft hier immer zu sagen scheint ...
(greift nach dem Hörer) Hallo Steve, kann ich kurz mit Ihnen sprechen?

Background Information

Painting the Forth Bridge ...

The Forth Bridge, spanning the estuary of the Forth River in Scotland, was a masterpiece of engineering when built in 1889. The iron bridge is a mile long and its cantilever structure is so large it has to be constantly repainted. No sooner have painters completed the job than they have to start again. Thus if any job of work is compared with painting the Forth Bridge it means the task is virtually endless.

Train Yourself

Setzen Sie das folgende Gespräch ins Passiv!

Beispiel: They told us yesterday – we were told by them yesterday

My company put the order in more than a month ago and they kept us waiting until today for delivery. The courier service delivered the package during our lunch break, so we were not able to check its contents immediately. When our sorting department opened the package they discovered that ATCO had sent the wrong product. We instructed the sorting department to contact you without delay, but your despatch department insisted they had sent the correct item.

Background Information

Commission or rebate?

»Commission« is a contractually-agreed percentage of the value of goods sold, paid to the seller – usually a sales representative – or his or her agent.

»Rebate« is a reduction in the sales price of any goods, usually made on bulk orders.
In American English, a »**commission house**« is a stockbroker's office that buys and sells stock for customers on a commission basis. A »**commission merchant**« is a person who buys or sells goods on behalf of others, receiving commission for his services.

Train Yourself

Finden Sie die passenden Wörter!

1. The company employed him on a ______ basis, and he had great success when he offered substantial ______ to his customers.
2. On orders in excess of 100,000 dollars we are able to offer a ______ of 15%. In view of the fact that our sales representatives are on 10% ______, we regard this as a very generous offer.
3. Although he is our top salesman we really can't offer him more than 15% ______, particularly as he has been offering customers such a generous ______.

Talk Talk Talk

P. Hi, Steve. I've had a letter of complaint that seems to belong in your **department**.

P. Hallo Steve, ich habe hier einen Beschwerdebrief, der zu Ihrer **Abteilung** zu gehören scheint.

S. Let's have a **look-see**! Hmm, something seems to have gone wrong somewhere, doesn't it?

S. Lassen Sie uns **einen Blick darauf werfen**. Hm, sieht aus, als wäre irgendwo irgendetwas schief gegangen, nicht wahr?

P. You're telling me! If we overlook inquiries like this we really could **lose a lot of business**.

P. Was Sie nicht sagen! Wenn wir Anfragen wie diese hier übersehen, könnten wir **eine Menge Aufträge verlieren**.

S. Frankly, I can't recall ever hearing from a company called Severn & Sons. Letters inquiring **about our products** are usually answered **on the turn. I'll check this out**.

S. Ehrlich gesagt kann ich mich nicht daran erinnern, schon mal was von einer Firma namens Severn & Sons gehört zu haben. Briefe, in denen man sich **nach unseren Produkten** erkundigt, werden normalerweise **sofort** beantwortet. **Ich werde dem nachgehen**.

P. Thanks, Steve. Before replying to the letter I would appreciate hearing if we ever got the original inquiry.

P. Danke Steve. Bevor ich antworte, hätte ich gerne gewusst, ob wir diese Anfrage wirklich jemals bekommen haben.

S. I might have a bit of a problem checking the correspondence received over the past month. But I'm sure Beryl will have no objection helping me out. But we can't rule out the possibility of the letter landing on the old man's desk and staying there. Perhaps he never got around to dealing with it himself.

S. Es dürfte schwierig werden, die Korrespondenz des letzten Monats zu überprüfen. Aber sicher wird Beryl nichts dagegen haben, mir zu helfen. Wir können die Möglichkeit nicht ausschließen, dass der Brief auf dem Schreibtisch des Alten gelandet und dort liegen geblieben ist. Vielleicht ist er nie dazu gekommen, sich selbst damit zu beschäftigen.

P. That's a possibility, of course. But let's start by checking your past correspondence.

P. Das ist natürlich eine Möglichkeit. Aber lassen Sie uns damit anfangen, die alte Korrespondenz durchzusehen.

S. No problem, Peter. I'll be starting on it just as soon as I've had my coffee.

S. Kein Problem, Peter. Ich werde gleich damit anfangen, wenn ich meinen Kaffee ausgetrunken habe.

Train Yourself

Was ist richtig? Das Gerund, der Infinitiv oder eine Kombination von Präposition und Gerund?

1. I really object *(have)* to do all this work alone.

   ....

2. It's no use *(object)* to the amount of work expected.

   ....

3. *(object)*, you should have first of all made sure what was expected.

   ....

4. I *(write ... inform)* you that the goods you ordered are now ready for dispatch. ....

5. *(inform)* us that the contract was ready *(sign)* they kept us waiting a further week. ....

6. We have great pleasure *(inform)* you that your order is ready for you *(collect)*. ....

7. *(order)* this item from your catalogue we forgot *(give)* the reference number. ....

8. We would like *(order)* 500 boxes of your company's Christmas crackers *(deliver)* by December 10. ....

9. *(order)* we would like first of all to know your conditions of sale.

   ....

10. We experienced problems *(contact)* you.

    ....

11. *(contact)* the company, we made sure we had their correct telephone number and address. ....

12. In order *(contact)* the company we had to call telephone inquiries to find out the right number. ....

Talk Talk Talk

(Peter's Office)

(Peters Büro)

P. Hello, Beryl! What can I do for you?

P. Hallo Beryl! Was kann ich für Sie tun?

B. Oh, Mr Brückner. **I'm very sorry to have to confess** that I've made a big **blunder**. Mr Morgan dictated to me a reply to that inquiry from Severn & Sons before he left for the seminar. He was in a hurry and I took a **notebook** I don't normally use. Afterwards, my attention was **diverted** by another task, and I quite forgot the letter. It was only when Mr Blackman asked me about it just now that I remembered. I just don't know how I made such a stupid mistake.

B. Oh Mr Brückner. **Es tut mir so Leid, es Ihnen sagen zu müssen**, aber ich habe mir einen großen **Patzer** geleistet. Mr Morgan hat mir eine Antwort auf die Anfrage von Severn & Sons diktiert, bevor er auf das Seminar gegangen ist. Er hatte es eilig und ich habe ein **Notizheft** genommen, das ich normalerweise nicht benutze. Danach ist meine Aufmerksamkeit auf etwas anderes **gelenkt** worden und ich habe den Brief fast vergessen. Erst als Mr Blackman mich eben danach fragte, fiel es mir wieder ein. Ich weiß gar nicht, wie mir so ein dummer Fehler passieren konnte.

P. Well, we all make mistakes, Beryl – I've made enough in my time. The biggest mistake of all is to try to cover one's mistakes up – and that mistake, at least, you did not make. I appreciate you coming so promptly to me, Beryl – we can **make up** a bit of **lost time** now. Where's that letter from Severn & Sons?

P. Tja, wir alle machen Fehler, Beryl – ich habe früher genug gemacht. Der größte Fehler ist es, zu versuchen den Fehler zu vertuschen – und diesen Fehler haben Sie wenigstens nicht gemacht. Ich finde es gut, dass sie sofort zu mir gekommen sind, Beryl – wir können jetzt einen Teil der **verlorenen Zeit wett machen.** Wo ist der Brief von Severn & Sons?

B. Mr Blackman's got it. He's ever so angry.

B. Den hat Mr Blackman. Er ist so was von wütend.

P. Anger isn't going to help us, Beryl. Get the letter – and get your notebook. But the right one, please!

P. Wut hilft uns nicht weiter, Beryl. Holen Sie den Brief – und ihr Notizheft. Aber bitte das richtige!

(Peter dictates a letter to Beryl ...)

(Peter diktiert Beryl einen Brief ...)

To Severn & Sons, Worcester
Dear Sirs,

Thank you for your letter of May 18, to which **we are replying as a matter of utmost priority**. **We are extremely concerned** that you have been waiting so long for a reply to your original request. **I must confess** that your original letter was unaccountably overlooked, an oversight for which we must sincerely apologise. I am personally arranging for the immediate dispatch by express post of a complete information package on AGIT. We are very pleased to hear the product has been recommended to you, and we can assure you it is the very best of its kind. **If you have any further queries please do not hesitate to contact me** on my office extension. **I am directing my personal attention to this matter.**

Yours faithfully,

Peter Brückner,
Assistant Managing Director

Train Yourself

Verbinden Sie die Wörter und Ausdrücke mit ähnlicher Bedeutung!

go wrong, query, hesitate, dispatch, overlook, rule out, blunder, check, normally, angry, make up, cover up, promptly, task

mistake, at once, question, malfunction, usually, furious, send, eliminate, job, put together, disguise, delay, fail to observe, examine

Talk Talk Talk

(Peter's office. Melissa enters)	(Peters Büro. Melissa kommt herein)
M. Have your ears been burning?	M. Haben Ihnen die Ohren gebrannt?
P. What do you mean?	P. Was meinen Sie damit?
M. Oh, it's an expression we have when somebody is talking about us.	M. Oh, den Ausdruck benutzen wir, wenn jemand über uns spricht.
P. I'm burning, all right – but burning to get home. I'm **dog-tired**.	P. Ich brenne, das stimmt – aber ich brenne darauf, nach Hause zu kommen. Ich bin **hundemüde**.
M. Peter, your English is now quite amazing. You could pass for an Englishman – well, almost.	M. Peter, Ihr Englisch ist schon ziemlich beeindruckend. Sie könnten als Engländer durchgehen – na ja, fast.
P. I'll keep the almost – I'm German and I don't want to forget it! But why should my ears be on fire?	P. Ich bleibe bei dem fast – ich bin Deutscher und das will ich nicht vergessen. Aber warum sollten meine Ohren in Flammen stehen?
M. Burning, Peter, Burning. You've won a big admirer.	M. Brennen, Peter, brennen. Sie haben eine große Bewunderin dazugewonnen.
P. Well, that's nice to hear. But tell me more. Who?	M. Na, das höre ich gerne. Erzählen Sie mir mehr davon. Wer?
M. Beryl.	M. Beryl.
P. Beryl! But I've just **given** her a **telling off**!	P. Beryl! Aber ich habe ihr gerade eine **Standpauke gehalten**.

M. No, that's the point. You didn't. At least, she tells me you didn't. She says you treated her mistake with great understanding.

M. Nein, darum geht es. Das haben Sie nicht getan. Zumindest sagt sie, Sie hätten das nicht getan. Sie sagt, dass Sie mit ihrem Fehler sehr verständnisvoll umgegangen sind.

P. Well, there's no **crying over spilt milk** – now that's something else I've learnt here in England.

P. Na ja, was passiert ist, ist passiert – das ist noch etwas, das ich in England gelernt habe.

M. But you could have made things very difficult for her.

M. Aber Sie hätten ihr große Schwierigkeiten machen können.

P. But why should I? What would that achieve? She won't make the mistake again. And the mistake was quite easy to correct.

P. Warum sollte ich? Was würde das bringen? Sie wird den Fehler nicht noch mal machen. Und dieser Fehler war leicht wieder gutzumachen.

M. Peter, you're on the way to becoming a very good manager!

M. Peter, Sie sind dabei, ein sehr guter Manager zu werden!

Train Yourself

1. Füllen Sie die Lücken in diesem Geschäftsbrief mit den richtigen Wörtern!

Dear Sirs,

I am writing to ______ your letter of September 21 and to ______ for the ______ delay in ______ the order ______ for the start of the Christmas season. The problem ______ in the late ______ of important ______ from our ______. We have ______ a complaint with them and ______ for a ______ in their quoted price. This, of course, we shall ______ directly on to you.
______ again for any ______ and ______ you of our best attention,
Yours ______,

forward, parts, assuring, pass, hope, suppliens, assuring, lay, arrival, acknowledge, regrettable, apologising, faithfully, discount, apologise, inconvenience, in time, lodged, dispatching.

2. Finden Sie das Gegenteil (Antonym) zum jeweiligen Wort:

1. late	insincere
2. delighted	easy
3. send	early
4. ask	right
5. sincere	depart
6. trust	forget
7. wrong	receive
8. difficult	reply
9. achieve	mistrust
10. remember	disappointed
11. arrive	fail

Talk Talk Talk

(Peter's office. James Morgan enters)

(Peters Büro. Mr Morgan kommt herein)

J. Good morning, Peter! Everything under control?

J. Guten Morgen, Peter! Alles unter Kontrolle?

P. Good morning, Mr Morgan. I think so. We had a couple of problems, problem letters – that kind of thing. But we sorted them out between us.

P. Guten Morgen, Mr Morgan. Ich denke schon. Wir hatten ein paar Probleme, problematische Briefe – und solche Sachen. Aber wir haben das unter uns ausgemacht.

J. Well done. Don't give me the details – I'm still recovering from that seminar. Three days of inten-

J. Gut gemacht. Erzählen Sie mir keine Einzelheiten – ich erhole mich gerade noch von dem

sive lectures. My head's spinning. Lucy, where's that coffee?

Seminar. Drei Tage voller intensiver Vorträge. Mein Kopf dreht sich. Lucy, wo bleibt der Kaffee?

L. Right here, Mr Morgan. My, you look really exhausted – can I get you a **pick-you-up**?

L. Hier, Mr Morgan. Sie sehen wirklich erschöpft aus, kann ich einen **Muntermacher** besorgen?

J. Not the kind I really need, Lucy. It's too early for alcohol! The coffee will help. Now, Peter, I **made some useful contacts** at the seminar, and I'd like you to follow up **some of the leads** for me.

J. Nicht die Art, die ich eigentlich bräuchte. Es ist zu früh für Alkohol! Der Kaffee wird helfen. Also, Peter, ich **habe** auf dem Seminar **ein paar nützliche Kontakte geknüpft** und möchte, dass Sie **ein paar der wichtigsten** für mich weiterverfolgen.

P. Certainly, Mr Morgan. How can I help?

P. Natürlich, Mr Morgan. Wie kann ich Ihnen helfen?

J. Two of the directors there represented very big companies and both expressed interest in the Accounting 2000 program. Can you write to them on my behalf giving them **background information**? I told them all I could, but we should get something to them in writing.

J. Zwei der Direktoren dort vertraten sehr große Firmen und beide zeigten Interesse am Accounting 2000-Programm. Könnten Sie ihnen in meinem Auftrag schreiben, um ihnen ein paar **Hintergrundinformationen** zu geben? Ich habe ihnen erzählt, was ich nur konnte, aber wir sollten ihnen etwas Schriftliches zukommen lassen.

P. Certainly, Mr Morgan …
Lucy, I'll have two letters for you on the **dictaphone** later today. Will you have time to type them up for me?

P. Natürlich, Mr Morgan …
Lucy, später habe ich auf dem **Diktiergerät** noch zwei Briefe für Sie. Werden Sie dann Zeit haben, sie für mich zu tippen?

L. No problem, Peter. I'll keep the afternoon free for you.

L. Kein Problem, Peter. Ich halte mir den Nachmittag für Sie frei.

P. Well, here goes ...

P. Also, los geht's ...

The first letter is to:

Mr Timothy Rogers,
Managing Director,
Newland Brokers Limited,
Basingstoke (I'll let you have the exact address later, Lucy!)

Dear Mr Rogers,

Our Managing Director, Mr James Morgan, has asked me to write to you to say how pleased he was to make your acquaintance at the managerial seminar last week in Brighton. He noted your interest in our software program Accounting 2000, which is my direct area of responsibility. Hence, **it is my pleasure to write to you** with a description of the program and some excerpts from the many testimonials and recommendations we have had from satisfied clients.
These include a letter from the North of England Land Recovery Service which is employing the Accounting 2000 system in every one of its 22 offices. The law company Spinks, Grobat and Renny has just installed the system in 12 of its subsidiary offices nationwide. You will find their testimonials among others in **Appendix** 2. The description of the program itself is attached as Appendix 1. Apart from these, we are taking the liberty of sending you ERGO's documentation on the Accounting 2000 system and our range of brochures.
If you have any further questions on the system please do not hesitate to call me on my direct line, or to write to me at the above address. Mr Morgan asks me to add his sincere greetings.

Yours sincerely,

Peter Brückner,
Assistant Managing Director,
ERGO Limited

P. The second letter, Lucy, is to Mr Thomas Rampton, of Rampton Industrial Machines. You'll find the address on his **letter-head** ...

P. Lucy, der zweite Brief geht an Mr Thomas Rampton von Rampton Industrial Machines. Die Adresse finden Sie auf dem **Briefkopf** ...

Dear Mr Rampton,

Our Managing Director, Mr James Morgan, has asked me to write to you **to express his appreciation for the extremely complimentary remarks you made to him**, at the managerial seminar, on the Accounting 2000 software program which we market.
He was sorry he did not have the opportunity or time to give you a full description of the program, and consequently he has asked me to send you the relevant information. Apart from documentation and brochures, I am sending you as **appendices** to this letter a brief outline of the program and its uses, and excerpts from letters of recommendation and testimonials. I have also taken the liberty of asking our Sales Department to instruct our representative in Derby to call you and, if you wish, make an appointment to make you personally more closely acquainted with the program. **Should you have any further questions or require additional information do not hesitate to contact me on my personal extension.**
Mr Morgan joins me in sending sincere greetings,

Yours sincerely,

Peter Brückner,
Assistant Managing Director

Background Information

Appendix - isn't that a useless body part?

»Appendix« has several meanings – and not only in the medical field. Apart from describing the small appendage of the large intestine, »appendix« means anything added – in business correspondence it describes any addition to the main letter, such as an additional sheet of paper containing extra information. The plural is appendices.

Recommendation or testimonial?

A recommendation in favour of a product can be either written or verbal - a testimonial is always in written form.

Train Yourself

Setzen Sie in den folgenden Sätzen die richtige Form ein:

1. The company sent a __________ placing on record its satisfaction with the product.
2. Acting on your __________ I wrote to the company asking for further information.
3. Thank you for the __________, which we have framed and put in a place of prominence at headquarters.

Talk Talk Talk

(Peter's office. A knock on the door)

(Peter Büro. Es klopft an der Tür)

P. Come in – oh, it's you Chip. What can I do for you?

P. Herein – ach, Sie sind es, Chip. Was kann ich für Sie tun?

C. I had to pick up this letter from Torrence and Partners in Cheapside. They said it was important – I'd give it to Mr Morgan, but he isn't here. Lucy said you should handle it.

C. Ich sollte diesen Brief von Torrence and Partners in Cheapside abholen. Sie sagten mir, es wäre wichtig – ich wollte ihn Mr Morgan geben, aber er ist nicht da. Lucy sagte, Sie sollten sich darum kümmern.

P. She's right. I'm handling most of Mr Morgan's correspondence, anyway. Let's see what this one is about.

P. Sie hat Recht. Ich kümmere mich sowieso um den Großteil von Mr Morgans Korrespondenz. Lassen Sie uns mal sehen, worum es hier geht.

C. Anything else, Mr Brückner?

C. Ist sonst noch was, Mr Brückner?

P. Yes, Chip – be a good chap and run out for a couple of sandwiches for me. I'll have to lunch at my desk today. And this may be one of the reasons, if it's that urgent ...

P. Ja, Chip, seien Sie ein netter Kerl und holen Sie mir ein paar Sandwiches. Ich werde heute am Schreibtisch zu Mittag essen müssen. Und das hier könnte einer der Gründe dafür sein, wenn es schon so dringend ist ...

Dear Sirs/Mesdames,

We are taking the liberty of returning to you by your company courier the Trigger software package which you delivered one week ago. There appears to be a fundamental fault which our computer specialist has been unable to rectify. We had no problem installing it but then had difficulty with the various configurations, which appear to be incompatible with our hardware. **We would be very pleased** if you checked the problem and informed us of the results of your investigation.
You will understand that we are withholding payment until the problem is solved.

Yours faithfully,

Charles Jospin,
p.p. Torrence and Partners

Background Information

p.p. at the foot of a letter is an abbreviation from the Latin »per procurationem«, meaning »officially acting for ...«
pp without the full-stops is an abbreviation for the word »pages«.
In informal correspondence, a **PS** (= postscript; an abbreviation of the Latinism Post Script) precedes an addition to the letter following the signature ...
With very best wishes,
John
PS I forgot to tell you that Henry and Maud are getting married in the summer.

And now for some other »P« abbreviations you will meet in official correspondence:

p.a. – per annum, or annually, yearly
PA – Personal Assistant
p.c. or **pct** – per cent
pd – paid
p/e – price-earnings ratio
PO – Post Office
PPS – Additional postscript (Post Post Script), used when an additional topic is addressed following the signature at the end of a letter
PR – Public Relations
PRO – Public Relations Officer
pro tem (abbreviation of the Latinism pro tempore) – for the time being (»He was appointed director pro tem«)
proximo – Latinism used in naming dates, meaning »of the next month« – (»The goods will be delivered on the 6th proximo, precisely on the 6th of March«). The opposite is »ultimo« – »The goods were delivered on the 20th ultimo« (meaning the preceding month).

Train Yourself

Der Schreiber des folgenden Briefes scheint die Abkürzungen, die er benutzt hat, durcheinander gebracht zu haben. **Können Sie die richtigen Formen finden?**

Dear Jack,

I have some good news for you. I've just been appointed *PO* of a big *PPS* company here in the city. I don't yet know what I'll be paid *PA*, but *pro forma* - or for the time being as they say - I'm happy. I am assured of a *p.c.* rise of 10 *p/e*, though. Give me a call some time and I'll tell you more.

Your good friend,
Jim

pps Can you make lunch next Tuesday?

Vocabulary

appendix - appendices (pl.)	Anhang
to assign	unterzeichnen
to be off-base	nicht da sein; außer Haus sein
to bin	weg werfen
to blind sb. with science	jdn. mit großen Worten beeindrucken
blunder	(schwerer) Fehler
brief	kurz
to chuck	zerknüllen
considerable	beachtlich
to divert	ablenken
dog-tired	hundemüde
do the trick	funktionieren
to give a telling off	eine Standpauke halten
grey zone	Grauzone
incompatible	unverträglich/unvereinbar
to junk	wegwerfen
to keep abreast of	Schritt halten mit
letter-head	Briefkopf
look-see	kurzer Blick
to make up lost time	verlorene Zeit aufholen
not to cry over spilt milk	»was passiert ist, ist passiert«
on the turn	sofort, umgehend
pick-you-up	Muntermacher
to propagate	verbreiten
to rectify	richtig stellen
referral	Vermittlung
to rubbish	mies/schlecht machen
sign on behalf of	im Auftrag von ... unterschreiben
some of the leads	ein paar der Wichtigsten
stinker	harter Brocken
to subcontract = to farm out	Unteraufträge vergeben
subtle	subtil/feinsinnig
testimonial	Anerkennung/(positive) Referenz
user-friendly	benutzerfreundlich

Offers

Angebote

Here we go

Neben den alltäglichen Dingen, die bei der Firmenkorrespondenz anfallen, wie Anfragen und Beschwerden, werden auf dem Postweg natürlich auch wichtige geschäftliche Verbindungen angebahnt. Peter bekommt von James Morgan die Aufgabe übertragen, sich um einen bedeutenden Franchise-Vertrag von ERGO Limited mit einem amerikanischen Softwareanbieter zu kümmern. Wird Peter es schaffen, diesen verantwortungsvollen Auftrag zur Zufriedenheit aller zu bewältigen?

Talk Talk Talk

(James Morgan's office)	(James Morgans Büro)
J. (speaks into telephone) Peter, could you step into my office, please!	J. (ins Telefon) Peter, könnten Sie bitte in mein Büro kommen?
P. (enters) Good morning, Mr Morgan. What can I do for you?	P. (tritt ein) Guten Morgen, Mr Morgan. Was kann ich für Sie tun?
J. I've been asked by **head office** in America to inquire into the possibility of obtaining a franchise for the United States for a new software product which Newcom in Manchester **has just brought out**. It was favourably written about in the American magazine *Computer World*. We might be too late, nevertheless head office wants us to go ahead and approach Newcom. I'm	J. Ich wurde vom **Hauptbüro** in Amerika darum gebeten, herauszufinden, ob es möglich ist, die amerikanischen Franchise Lizenzen einer neuen Software zu erwerben, die Newcom in Manchester **gerade herausgebracht hat**. In dem amerikanischen Magazin *Computer World* wurde sehr positiv darüber berichtet. Wir kommen damit vielleicht schon zu spät, aber das

really under pressure this week, therefore I'd like you to take this one over for me.

Hauptbüro möchte trotzdem, dass wir es versuchen und Newcom ansprechen. Ich bin diese Woche wirklich ziemlich im Stress, deswegen hätte ich gern, dass Sie die Sache für mich übernehmen.

P. Certainly, Mr Morgan.

P. Natürlich, Mr Morgan.

J. Head office faxed us the *Computer World* article. You'll find everything you need there – even the address of Newcom and the name of their **Project Manager**. I'd be glad if you could get on to it right away ...

J. Das Hauptbüro hat uns den Artikel aus der *Computer World* gefaxt. Sie finden darin alles, was Sie brauchen – selbst die Adresse von Newcom und den Namen ihres **Projektmanagers**. Es wäre schön, wenn Sie sich gleich darum kümmern könnten ...

Train Yourself

»Therefore« oder »nevertheless«?

Setzen Sie das richtige Wort in die folgenden Sätze ein!

1. We experienced delays in deliveries from our suppliers, ________ we were unable to complete your order in time.
2. Our production line let us down badly, ________ we shall do everything possible to get the goods to you by the end of next week.
3. We regret that we have not yet received payment for the last shipment, ________ we are not yet processing your second order.
4. Although we are far from happy with the performance of the C-100 model, we shall ________ continue to work with it during its trial period.

Background Information

»Nevertheless« is often – and particularly in written English – replaced by »nonetheless« or (but more rarely) »notwithstanding«. **»Notwithstanding«** has the same meaning as despite – but has the

distinction of normally »standing« at the start of the sentence ...
Notwithstanding (or despite) his objections, the company went ahead with its rationalization program. The company went ahead with its rationalization program despite his objections.
»Notwithstanding« is very rarely used in spoken English but is nevertheless often found in formal business correspondence.

Talk Talk Talk

(Peter dictates a letter to Newcom)	(Peter diktiert einen Brief an Newcom)
P. This letter is to Mr Trevor Payne, Project Manager of Newcom Technology – Lucy, you have the address on the fax.	P. Dieser Brief geht an Mr Trevor Payne, Projektmanager von Newcom Technology – Lucy, die Adresse finden Sie auf dem Fax.

Dear Mr Payne,

Our attention was caught by the article on your company's software program »Instantweb«, which was carried by the American magazine Computer World. ERGO Limited markets in the United States and Britain a wide range of software products, including a successful newspaper copy-editing program which might well be complemented by »Instantweb«. In combination, the two programs could contribute to an easier and more rapid access to the Internet by newspaper editorial offices.
Our head office in the United States was particularly interested in this possibility and we **have been asked to approach you** with a view to obtaining the franchise for »Instantweb« in the United States. If the franchise is still available, we would be pleased to discuss with you all relevant details with a view to reaching a business contract of benefit to both enterprises.
I look forward to hearing from you,
Yours sincerely,

Peter Brückner,
Assistant Managing Director

Background Information

»**Franchise**« or »**licence**«?

A »franchise« is an official, contractual authorization to sell a company's products or services in a specified region or country.

A »licence« is the document of authorization.

Train Yourself

1. Im vorhergehenden Brief hat Peter einige Schlüsselsätze in der Passivform geschrieben. Das Aktiv ist jedoch dem Passiv immer vorzuziehen – **also helfen Sie ihm und korrigieren Sie seinen Brief!**

2. Die Konjunktionen *and, but, because, since*.

Verbinden Sie jeden der folgenden Satzteile damit!

1. We intend placing an order for items 1, 3 and 6 ________ first of all we would like to see your full price list.
2. We would like to order 100 units ________ look forward to a prompt delivery.
3. We regret having to return the delivered goods ________ they arrived in a spoilt condition.
4. We regretfully have to cancel the contract ________ you failed to honour an important clause.
5. We would normally have cancelled the contract ________ we recognize you acted in good faith.
6. Thank you for your prompt reply ________ we look forward to a fruitful co-operation.

Talk Talk Talk

(James Morgan's office. Peter enters)

(James Morgans Büro. Peter tritt ein)

P. Good morning, Mr Morgan. I'm afraid the reply from Newcom doesn't look very promising.

P. Guten Morgen, Mr Morgan. Ich fürchte, die Antwort von Newcom hört sich nicht sehr viel versprechend an.

J. Let me see the letter ...

J. Zeigen Sie mir mal den Brief ...

Dear Mr Brückner,

Thank you for your letter of May 21. **We were naturally pleased to hear that** our new software program »Instantweb« had caught not only the attention of »Computer World« but of your company, too.

Because of the »Computer World« publicity, we have received approaches from various companies and are at this time **involved in negotiations** with some of them. Nonetheless, we are not ruling out your company, and would certainly welcome your more detailed proposals on a possible franchise for the United States.

Yours sincerely,

Trevor Payne

J. Hmm, how do we **take it from here**?

J. Hmmm, wie sollen wir jetzt **weiter vorgehen**?

P. Well, as I see it, we have to convince them that we are the right company for the franchise. But how?

P. Nun ja, so wie ich das sehe, müssen wir sie überzeugen, dass wir die richtige Firma für ein Franchise sind. Aber wie?

J. Peter, let me think this one over, and I'll come back to you on it ...

J. Peter, lassen Sie mich über diese Sache nachdenken, ich komme dann wieder auf Sie zu ...

Train Yourself

1. »Cost« or »price«? **Füllen Sie die Lücken mit den richtigen Wörtern!**

1. Would you please send us your current ______ list.
2. We can't afford to pay such a high ______.
3. Production ______ were too high for the project to be a success.
4. We were able to keep ______ stable by cutting production ______.
5. The ______ is as stated. It would push our ______ to an intolerable level if we cut ______ any further.
6. If the ______ is right, my recommendation is to buy. The ______ to you is low compared to what you can make on the deal.

2. Peter muss drei dringliche Geschäftsbriefe beantworten. Beachten Sie dabei besonders den Gebrauch der Wörter »consequent« und »consequence«.

1.
Dear Sirs/Mesdames,

Our accountants inform me that a mistake in our costing department has resulted in a credit in your favour amounting to $2,560. **Consequently**, we have pleasure in sending you forthwith a cheque in this amount ...

2.
Dear John,

Our conversation over dinner last night has given me food (no pun intended!) for thought. As a **consequence**, I'd like to put to you the following business proposition ...

3.
Sirs,

I have the unpleasant task of informing you that your company's failure to live up to the terms of the contract will have legal **consequences** ...

Finden Sie nun die richtige Form im folgenden Lückentext:

1. May we remind you of the legal ______ that may arise as a result of your actions?
2. We have waited two weeks for a reply to our letter, ______ we have no alternative but to look elsewhere.
3. ______ to our last letter, and as a result of your latest offer, we are now able to place an order for 2,000 items.
4. We were most impressed by the results of the pilot project, ______ we have pleasure in placing an immediate order.

False Friends

The English word **»consequent«** has nothing at all in common with German »konsequent«. »Consequent« and **»consequence«** both describe anything that logically follows something else, the result of a previous happening or action.
So, in the above example, numbered 1, Peter writes that as a consequence – as a result – of an error in the costing department, his company is able to repay a sum of $2,500. In example 2, he informs John that as a consequence – as a result – of their dinner conversation he is able to make a business proposition. In example 3, he informs a company that failure to live up to contractual obligations will have legal consequences – will result in legal action.

Talk Talk Talk

(John Morgan's office)

J. Peter, I think the only way to tackle the Newcom issue is to make a **personal visit**. I don't

(John Morgans Büro)

J. Peter, ich glaube, der einzige Weg, diese Newcom-Geschichte richtig anzugehen, ist ein **persön-**

think any amount of letter-writing is going to solve this one.

licher Besuch. Ich denke, ein noch so großer Haufen Briefe wird uns in dieser Angelegenheit nicht weiterbringen.

P. I **tend to** agree, but who should attempt it – Steve?

P. Ich **neige dazu**, Ihnen zuzustimmen, aber wer soll das versuchen – Steve?

J. Steve's a good **sales director**. But this isn't a sale – it's a much more complicated matter.

J. Steve ist ein guter **Verkaufsleiter**. Aber hier geht es nicht um einen Verkauf – das ist eine viel kompliziertere Angelegenheit.

P. So who have we got?

P. Wen haben wir denn sonst noch?

J. You, Peter. You!

J. Sie, Peter. Sie!

P. Me. A **franchise contract**? I hardly know what a franchise is!

P. Mich? Für einen **Franchise-Vertrag**? Ich weiß ja kaum, was ein Franchise ist!

J. I know we haven't spent a lot of time together, but I have observed one thing – you are very quick to learn, Peter. I'll give you three days to **swot** this subject up – and then Newcom is all yours!

J. Ich weiß, dass wir uns noch nicht lange kennen, aber eins ist mir aufgefallen – Sie lernen schnell, Peter. Ich gebe Ihnen drei Tage, um sich in dieser Sache **schlau zu machen –** und dann gehört Newcom Ihnen!

P. Oh, no! And if I don't succeed?

P. Oh, nein! Und wenn ich keinen Erfolg habe?

J. Steve tells me he has an opening in sales!

J. Steve hat mir gesagt, er hätte noch eine offene Stelle im Verkauf!

Train Yourself

»Swot« ist ein Slang-Ausdruck und bedeutet »intensiv lernen«. **Finden Sie für die nun folgenden Slang-Ausdrücke und umgangssprachlichen Wörter formellere Begriffe:**

1. There wasn't much to learn about the product. I got the **gist** of it in no time.
2. If you give me the **gen** I'll read up on the product at home tonight.
3. Give me the papers. I'd like to **take a look-see at** them.
4. I gave him the **low-down** on the terms of the contract.
5. Let's **gen** ourselves **up** on the background of the company before the meeting.
6. Just give me the **guts** of what the report has to say.

Alternativen:
examine, basic facts, information, inform, essence, inside information.

Talk Talk Talk

(Peter's office)

P. I have an important letter for you, Lucy. Could you bring your notebook – and a cup of your excellent tea, if it's not too much trouble.

L. Certainly, Peter. I'll be right there …

P. The letter is to Mr Trevor Payne, Project Manager of Newcom Technology, Birmingham. You have the exact address **on file**, Lucy …

(Peters Büro)

P. Ich muss Ihnen einen wichtigen Brief diktieren, Lucy. Könnten Sie bitte Ihr Notizbuch mitbringen – und vielleicht eine Tasse Tee, wenn es nicht zu viel Mühe macht.

L. Natürlich, Peter. Ich komme sofort …

P. Der Brief geht an Mr Trevor Payne, Projektmanager von Newcom Technology, Birmingham. Die exakte Adresse haben Sie **in Ihren Unterlagen**, Lucy …

Dear Mr Payne,

Thank you for your letter of May 26. **We fully understand** that other companies have also expressed interest in the »Instantweb« program, **but we are confident that we are best placed to give it the fullest market exposure** in the United States. We have various ideas on how this could be achieved within the framework of a franchise agreement, and I would be very pleased to explain these to you in a personal meeting. **I would be only too happy** to travel to your offices in Manchester on any day of your choosing and shall keep my diary free for the next two or three weeks in anticipation of a favourable reply from you.
Looking forward to hearing from you,

Yours sincerely,

Peter Brückner

P. Lucy, could you give a copy of that to Mr Morgan, and if he has no alterations to make then could you send it today by express post to Newcom?

P. Lucy, könnten Sie Mr Morgan eine Kopie davon geben und den Brief, wenn er keine Änderungen mehr vornehmen will, noch heute per Express an Newcom schicken?

L. Certainly, Peter.

L. Aber sicher, Peter.

(James Morgan enters Peter's office)

(James Morgan betritt Peters Büro)

J. Peter, the letter is fine. I've asked Lucy to send it right away. Now, I want to give you this – it's the **current annual report** of Newcom. It will **put** you **in the picture** – it's always best to know as much as you can about the company you're dealing with. If there's anything that's new to you or that

J. Peter, der Brief ist sehr gut. Ich habe Lucy gebeten, ihn sofort abzuschicken. Jetzt möchte ich Ihnen dies hier geben – das ist der **aktuelle Jahresbericht** von Newcom. Er wird sie **ins Bild setzen** – es ist immer gut, so viel wie möglich über die Firma zu wissen, mit der man es zu tun hat. Wenn es irgendetwas

you can't understand just let me know.	gibt, das neu für Sie ist oder das Sie nicht verstehen, lassen Sie es mich einfach wissen.

Background Information

An »**annual report**« is a full account of a company's activities over the previous year. It contains a balance sheet showing income, expenditure and the value of company assets. The final balance shows either a profit or loss and calculates a dividend payable to the company's shareholders. The annual report is presented at the annual meeting of shareholders, at which company officers also stand for re-election.

Train Yourself

Peter ist sich immer noch nicht so ganz sicher, wie er mit den Begriffen aus dem Jahresbericht von Newcom umgehen soll. **Können Sie ihm helfen, die Bedeutung der folgenden Wörter richtig zuzuordnen?**

1. balance sheet
2. board of directors
3. chief executive
4. current assets
5. multinational
6. profit and loss account
7. subsidiaries
8. supervisory board

a. A statement showing a company's expenditure and income over a period of usually one year.
b. A company's total wealth, in terms not only of cash, cheques and payments due, but property, equipment, stocks of goods, raw materials, etc.
c. A body of elected officers who run the company and who stand for re-election at the annual meeting.
d. A company's additional, semi-autonomous offices, usually distributed in various different countries.

e. When a company has such a network of offices abroad it is referred to in this way.
f. A financial statement showing a company's income, expenditures, assets and debts.
g. A small group of officers whose job is to overlook the work of the Board of Directors.
h. The head of a company's Board of Directors.

Background Information

»**Net**« or »**Gross**«?

In financial transactions and statements, »net« describes an amount entirely free of taxes, deductions, expenses etc. A company's net profit, for instance, is the amount of income remaining after deduction of all costs and expenses incurred in the production process. »Gross« has the opposite meaning, describing the total of anything, the result before deductions. A company's **gross profit**, for instance, is the total amount earned before taxes and other deductions.
And **gross national product**? That's the annual total value of goods produced and services provided by an individual country. The gross national product of South Africa in the year following the fall of apartheid there was equivalent to 75 billion American dollars.
This figure (usually abbreviated to GNP) is often expressed in »**per capita**« (»per head«) terms. South Africa has a population of 31 million – therefore the GNP »per capita« in the relevant period was equivalent to 2,400 American dollars.

Talk Talk Talk

(The offices of ERGO Limited)

(In den Büros von ERGO Limited)

L. Good morning, Peter. What a lovely day! Perhaps summer really is on the way. I have **a stack of** post for you!

L. Guten Morgen, Peter. Was für ein wunderbarer Tag! Vielleicht wird es wirklich langsam Sommer. Ich habe **einen ganzen Haufen** Post für Sie!

P. Thanks, Lucy. A pot of tea would also be welcome. And do you have any more of those biscuits your sister makes?

P. Danke, Lucy. Eine Tasse Tee wäre mir auch sehr recht. Und haben Sie vielleicht noch ein paar von diesen Keksen, die Ihre Schwester macht?

L. I kept some specially for you. Now you just take this **bundle** off to your office and I'll bring you tea **in a jiffy**.

L. Ich habe extra für Sie ein paar aufgehoben. Nehmen Sie diesen **Packen** hier einfach mit in Ihr Büro und ich bringe Ihnen **in Windeseile** Ihren Tee.

P. Lucy, you're a treasure.

P. Lucy, Sie sind ein Schatz.

(Melissa enters)
M. *»Schatz«* is the word! Don't you listen to his sweet words, Lucy. He's a German charmer!

(Melissa tritt ein)
M. Ein »Schatz«, ja? Hören Sie nicht auf Ihn, Lucy. Er ist ein deutscher Charmeur!

P. I **met my match** when I tried to charm you, though, Melissa!

P. Ich habe **mir die Zähne ausgebissen**, als ich versucht habe, meinen Charme bei Ihnen wirken zu lassen, Melissa!

M. Well, perhaps I can't make tea like Lucy. I certainly can't make biscuits like her sister!

M. Tja, vielleicht kann ich nicht so gut Tee kochen wie Lucy. Und ganz sicher backe ich nicht so gute Kekse wie ihre Schwester!

P. But you can serve up a marvellous English roast. Steve and I really enjoyed our meal with you.

P. Aber dafür servieren Sie einen wunderbaren englischen Braten. Steve und ich haben das Essen mit Ihnen wirklich genossen.

M. Well, if you're a good boy we might just repeat the experience. Now, off to work with you!

M. Nun ja, wenn Sie immer schön brav sind, können wir dieses Erlebnis ja noch einmal wiederholen. Und jetzt an die Arbeit!

P. I'm just sorting my post now – here's a reply from Newcom ...

P. Ich sortiere gerade meine Post – hier ist eine Antwort von Newcom ...

Dear Mr Brückner,

Thank you for your letter of June 2. I would be very happy to meet you at our offices here in Manchester on any day convenient to you next week to discuss franchise possibilities. **I would suggest a morning meeting** to allow us to continue the discussions over lunch and possibly into the afternoon. You would naturally be our guest for the entire day.
May I suggest that you call my secretary on the above extension to fix a day. If you require hotel accommodation in Manchester she will also be glad to accommodate your requirements.
Looking forward to meeting you and to fruitful discussions,

Yours sincerely,

Trevor Payne

Train Yourself

Multiple Choice. **Finden Sie die Lösung, die am besten passt:**

1. My secretary will be glad to __________ an appointment for you.
a. find
b. arrange
c. date

2. If you __________ hotel accommodation please don't hesitate to let us know.
a. require
b. seek
c. demand

3. We would be very glad to ______ your flight from London to Birmingham.

a. organize
b. find
c. book

Talk Talk Talk

(Peter's office)

P. Lucy, could you put me through to Newcom, please? You have the number.

L. Certainly, Peter. Just one moment.

P. Hello, Newcom? **Could you put me through** please to extension 210. Hello, is that Mr Payne's office? It's Peter Brückner of ERGO Limited here. Mr Payne wrote to me to suggest that I make an appointment for a meeting next week. Next Thursday? Fine. At 11 AM? Yes, that suits me very well. No, I don't need hotel accommodation. I shall return to London the same day. Should I fax you **confirmation of my travel arrangements**? No? I'll do it all the same – I like to have these things on file. But thank you very much for all your help. I look forward to my visit to Newcom …

(Peters Büro)

P. Lucy, könnten Sie mich bitte zu Newcom durchstellen? Die Nummer haben Sie.

L. Natürlich, Peter. Einen Moment bitte.

P. Hallo, Newcom? **Könnten Sie mich bitte** mit der Durchwahl -210 **verbinden**? Hallo, bin ich verbunden mit Mr Paynes Büro? Hier spricht Peter Brückner von ERGO Limited. Mr Payne hat mir geschrieben, um einen Termin für die nächste Woche vorzuschlagen. Nächsten Donnerstag? Sehr schön. Um 11 Uhr? Ja, das passt mir sehr gut. Nein, ich brauche keine Hotelreservierung. Ich reise noch am selben Tag nach London zurück. Soll ich Ihnen eine **Bestätigung für die Details meiner Reise zufaxen**? Nein? Ich tue es trotzdem – ich habe so etwas immer gern schriftlich. Aber vielen Dank für Ihre Hilfe. Ich freue mich schon auf meinen Besuch bei Newcom …

Fax to:

Mr Trevor Payne,
Projects Manager,
Newcom,

Manchester

From:
Peter Brückner,
Assistant Managing, Director
ERGO Limited,
London
Fax Nr. 003
Date: 04.06.2007

Dear Mr Payne,

This fax serves as confirmation that I will be travelling to Manchester next Thursday morning for a meeting with you at Newcom headquarters at 11 AM. Thank you very much for finding the time for a meeting, to which I look forward very much.

Yours truly,

Peter Brückner

Train Yourself

Einladungen - **Was gehört in die Lücken?**

1. If it is __________ for you, may I __________ you for tea at the Dorchester next Tuesday afternoon at 4?
2. To __________ the 25th anniversary of the company, we are __________ all employees to a champagne __________ in the conference room next Wednesday at 12 noon.

3. I would be very ______ if you and Mrs Smith accepted our ______ to dinner on the 25th. Cocktails at 7 PM.
4. Thank you for your ______ invitation to ______ the concert and supper-reception. My wife and I are very ______ to accept.
5. May we have the ______ of your ______ at dinner at the Ritz next Saturday?
6. Thank you so much for the invitation, but I'm ______ I am otherwise ______ on that evening.

honour, inviting, invitation, pleased, engaged, convenient, glad, kind, company, mark, reception, attend, afraid, invite.

Talk Talk Talk

(Peter's office, John Morgan enters)

(Peters Büro, John Morgan tritt ein)

J. Well, Peter, all **geared up** for the Manchester meeting?

J. Nun, Peter, **alles bereit** für das Meeting in Manchester?

P. I'm as ready as I ever shall be, Mr Morgan.

P. Ich bin so bereit, wie ich nur sein kann, Mr Morgan.

J. Any questions before you set off? You've got an early start tomorrow and we won't be seeing each other before then. I have to leave the office in ten minutes.

J. Noch irgendwelche Fragen, bevor Sie losfahren? Sie müssen morgen früh los und wir werden uns davor nicht mehr sehen. Ich muss in zehn Minuten das Büro verlassen.

P. No, I think I shall be all right, Mr Morgan.

P. Nein, ich glaube, ich komme schon klar, Mr Morgan.

J. Then good luck, Peter. See you the day after tomorrow ...

J. Dann viel Glück, Peter. Wir sehen uns dann übermorgen ...

(Melissa enters after a while)

(Etwas später tritt Melissa ein)

M. You're off to Manchester tomorrow, then, Peter?

M. Sie brechen also morgen nach Manchester auf, Peter?

P. That's right. Wish me luck!

P. Stimmt. Wünschen Sie mir Glück!

M. I'll do better than that. Come on, I'll buy you one at the *Nag's Head* – one for the road.

M. Ich werde noch etwas viel Besseres tun. Kommen Sie, ich lade Sie auf einen Drink im *Nag's Head* ein – einen für unterwegs.

P. Actually, I might just have two – but that's very kind of you, Melissa. I accept **unconditionally**. But what about Steve?

P. Vielleicht nehme ich sogar zwei – aber das ist wirklich sehr nett von Ihnen, Melissa. Ich nehme **ohne zu zögern** an. Aber was ist mit Steve?

M. No, I want you all to myself for half an hour Peter – I want to make sure you're prepared for what awaits you in Manchester. I've had some dealings in the past with Newcom. They're tough customers.

M. Nein, ich möchte Sie für ein halbes Stündchen ganz für mich allein haben, Peter – ich möchte sicher sein, dass Sie auf das, was Sie in Manchester erwartet, auch gut vorbereitet sind. Ich hatte in der Vergangenheit schon öfter mit Newcom zu tun. Das sind schwierige Kunden.

Train Yourself

1. James Morgan befragt Peter. **Setzen Sie in die Fragen jeweils »some« oder »any« ein:**

1. Did you make ______ progress at the meeting?
2. Could you give me ______ advice on how to tackle the problem?
3. I could only find ______ entries in an old calendar.
4. I'd like to open the meeting to a general discussion of the issue and ask if there are ______ questions.
5. Did the theatre production give you ______ pleasure at all?

6. I was able to get _______ meaning out of it.
7. Is there _______ sense at all in that book? Well, I did find _______ things of interest.
8. _______ of the points in his lecture I found quite provocative.

2. Wählen Sie nun zwischen »something« oder »anything«:

1. Have you _______ on your mind?
2. Do you have _______ at all in that forgetful head of yours?
3. Would you like to see _______ of the castle and grounds?
4. I can't see _______ at all from where I'm standing.
5. May I ask you _______ very important?
6. Ask me _______ at all, I really don't mind.
7. Was there _______ left over from the buffet after the guests had gone?
8. Did you have _______ to eat on the plane?

Talk Talk Talk

(Peter's Office)

P. Lucy, I have one important letter I must send before leaving for Manchester.

L. I'll be with you after I've made this one call, Peter.

P. I'll dictate it into the dictaphone, Lucy. Take your time.

(Peters Büro)

P. Lucy, ich habe hier noch einen sehr wichtigen Brief, den ich abschicken muss, bevor ich nach Manchester fahre.

L. Ich komme sofort zu Ihnen, nachdem ich diesen Anruf erledigt habe, Peter.

P. Ich spreche ihn einfach auf das Diktiergerät, Lucy. Lassen Sie sich Zeit.

To Longdale and Partners,
13 Palmeston Road,
Epsom.

(Lucy, fill in the exact postal code for me from the letter-head, please)

Dear Sirs,
Thank you for your inquiry about our Accounting 2000 Program. **I am arranging for you to receive all our available information on the system and for our regional sales representative**, Mr Simon Tucker, to call you and arrange for a meeting at which he will be happy to explain its qualities and functions and answer your questions.
Before contacting Mr Tucker, however, it would be useful for me to know the size of your accounting department and the nature of the accounting system you are now using. I shall be away for the next few days, but during my absence please feel free to contact our Sales Director, Mr Steve Blackman, who will be happy to answer any queries you may have.
Assuring you of my company's best attentions,

Yours faithfully,

Peter Brückner,
Assistant Managing Director

Train Yourself

Before, after, during, while, meanwhile ...

Geben Sie die richtige Präposition und die richtige Verbform an:

1. ______________ *(reply)* in full to your letter, I would like to remind you of one or two relevant facts.
2. It was only ______________ *(read)* your letter that I became aware of the true state of the company's affairs.
3. ______________ the time it took you *(reply)* I was able to find answers to all my questions.

4. I must confess that I read your letter only __________ *(receive)* the subsequent reminder.
5. __________ *(agree)* in principle to your proposals, I must raise one or two objections.
6. __________ *(examine)* your proposals, I shall respond in full; __________ please allow me a little time to study the situation.
7. __________ my time with the company, he __________ *(learn)* a surprising amount.
8. __________ *(leave)*, I would just like to thank you for your splendid hospitality.
9. Here is the proposal. Please study it __________ we *(wait)* in the Garibaldi Restaurant.
10. __________ *(study)* the proposal, I believe my company is in the position of being able to accept it.

Talk Talk Talk

(Peter prepares to leave the office. Lucy calls him back)	(Peter will gerade das Büro verlassen, als Lucy ihn zurückruft)
L. Oh, Peter! In this morning's post there was another letter from Longdale and Partners, which might **affect** your reply. I opened it because it was simply addressed to ERGO – but I think you should read it.	L. Oh, Peter! In der Post von heute Morgen war ein Brief von Longdale and Partners, der **Auswirkungen** auf Ihre Rückantwort **haben** könnte. Ich habe ihn geöffnet, weil er nur an ERGO adressiert war – aber ich glaube, Sie sollten ihn besser lesen.
P. Lucy, I'm off to lunch now but give me the letter and I'll read it in my break.	P. Lucy, ich bin gerade auf dem Weg zum Mittagessen, aber geben Sie mir einfach den Brief und ich lese ihn in meiner Pause.
L. Here it is. Are you having lunch with Miss Walker? She's already left, but she said she thought you were joining her.	L. Hier ist er. Gehen Sie mit Miss Walker zum Lunch? Sie ist schon gegangen, aber sagte, dass sie dachte, Sie würden mitkommen.

P. Yes, Lucy, that's why I'm in such a hurry. See you later ...

P. Ja, Lucy, deshalb habe ich es ja auch so eilig. Bis später ...

(At the *Nag's Head*)

(Im *Nag's Head)*

P. Hello, Melissa. Sorry I'm late but Lucy had an important letter to give to me.

P. Hallo, Melissa. Tut mir Leid, dass ich so spät komme, aber Lucy hat mir noch einen wichtigen Brief gegeben.

M. Important? Who from?

M. Wichtig? Von wem?

P. Longdale and Partners. They are interested in our Accounting 2000 program. It would be **a very important sale** for us.

P. Longdale and Partners. Sie sind an unserem Accounting 2000-Programm interessiert. Das wäre **ein sehr wichtiger Verkaufserfolg** für uns.

M. So what does the letter say?

M. Also, was steht in dem Brief?

Dear Sirs, Mesdames,

Subsequent to our letter of June 6, requesting full information on your Accounting 2000 system, we have been approached by Redstar Technologies with a very attractive offer which will undoubtedly have an **effect** on our final decision. **In all fairness to your company, we do not want to take this decision before comparing the various systems on offer**. Our problem is that the Redstar Technologies offer combines a highly **competitive price with a firm deadline** for our decision. We normally resist pressure of this kind, but the attractive nature of the offer compels us to take rapid action. Would your company be in the position of demonstrating to us your Accounting 2000 system within one week of receipt of this letter? In the meantime, you could perhaps fax us relevant information on the system. **Additionally**, we would appreciate a call establishing direct communication between our accounting department and whoever is responsible in your company for the Accounting

2000 system. Our Chief Accountant, Mr Francis Staff, can be reached on extension 4435 (Fax. 2965-4436).

Thanking you in advance for your prompt attention to this matter,

Yours faithfully,

Matthew Gilpin,
Chief Executive

False Friends

Be careful not to confuse **»affect«** and **»effect«**. The words are so similar that even the British have problems with them. »Affect« is most commonly used as a verb and »effect« is frequently the corresponding noun (although, to add to the confusion, it can also be used as a verb, meaning to bring about or accomplish something). To affect means to produce a result, a change or an »effect«. Mr Gilpin of Longdale and Partners says the offer from Redstar Technologies will inevitably **affect** his company's decision - will inevitably **have an effect** on it.

Train Yourself

»Affect« oder »effect«?

1. Alcohol has a very strange ________ on some people.
2. How will the downturn in profits ________ the company's future?
3. What ________ is Jim's promotion likely to have on his family?
4. Will the move to company headquarters in New York ________ his future plans?
5. How can we ________ this staff reshuffle without causing problems?
6. If you can ________ this plan successfully you're assured of promotion.
7. The ________ of the company move were quite unforeseen.
8. How is the Stock Market slump likely to ________ exports?
9. How can we ________ an export drive successfully?
10. The ________ of the reorganization are still to be felt.

Talk Talk Talk

(in the pub – continued ...)

(im Pub – Fortsetzung ...)

P. Well, Melissa, what do you make of that?

P. Tja, Melissa, was halten Sie davon?

M. Well, I wouldn't worry your head about it. You've got **bigger fish to fry**. This is Steve's problem.

M. Na ja, ich würde mir deshalb nicht den Kopf zerbrechen. Sie haben **einen größeren Fisch am Haken**. Das ist Steves Problem.

P. But he's not around.

P. Aber er ist nicht da.

M. He's back tomorrow.

M. Er kommt morgen zurück.

P. But I'm in Manchester.

P. Aber ich bin in Manchester.

M. Then I'll give him the correspondence.

M. Dann werde ich ihm die Korrespondenz geben.

P. You're a treasure. Another drink?

P. Sie sind ein Schatz. Noch einen Drink?

Do's and Don'ts

Matthew Gilpin of Longdale and Partners begins his letter: **»Subsequent to ...«**. He could have just as well written: **»After sending you our letter of ...«**. English stylists actually prefer the latter version, arguing that it is simpler and easier to understand. In spoken English, »subsequent to« virtually never occurs, but it is a very entrenched form in official letter-writing - whatever the »stylists« say! Equally, **»Thank you for your letter of ...«** is often replaced by a very formal **»We acknowledge receipt of your letter of ...«** or **»We are in receipt of your letter of ...«**. The two forms are in common use, but you will be never wrong in writing a simple: **»Thank you for your letter of ...«**

Train Yourself

Sie müssen einen Brief beantworten, in dem nach Informationen über ein neues Produkt gefragt wird, für das Ihre Firma wirbt. **Wie beginnen Sie Ihren Brief? Machen Sie mindestens drei Entwürfe und benutzen Sie jeweils die folgenden Wörter: »pleased«, »pleasure« und »glad«.**

....

....

....

Vocabulary

to affect	beeinflussen
bundle	Bündel/Packen
confirmation	Bestätigung
effect	Auswirkung
(to be) geared up	bereit sein (etwa: seine Siebensachen zusammen haben)
gross profit	Bruttogewinn
gross national product (GNP)	Bruttosozialprodukt
to have bigger fish to fry	einen größeren Fisch am Haken haben (etwas Wichtigeres vorhaben)
in a jiffy	im Handumdrehen/in «Windeseile«
in the picture	im Bild sein/Bescheid wissen
market exposure	Markteinführung
to meet one's match	»seinen Meister treffen«
on file	in den Unterlagen
per capita	pro Kopf
sales director	Verkaufsleiter
(a) stack of	ein ganzer Haufen (von)
stock	Vorrat
to swot (colloquial)	«büffeln; pauken» (ugs.)
to take it from here	jetzt weiter vorgehen
to tend to	dazu tendieren/neigen
unconditionally	bedingungslos/ohne Vorbehalte

Letter of application
Bewerbungsschreiben

Here we go

ERGO Limited ist auf der Suche nach einem neuen Mitarbeiter für die Marketingabteilung und hat aus diesem Grund eine Stellenanzeige in einer Zeitung geschaltet. Schnell treffen die ersten Bewerbungen bei der Firma ein und müssen nun sorgfältig geprüft und ausgewertet werden, und Mr Morgan ist davon überzeugt, dass Peter hierfür genau der richtige Mann ist ...

Talk Talk Talk

(Peter enters the office)

(Peter betritt das Büro)

L. Well, hello, Peter! **Did you have a successful journey** to Manchester?

L. Na so was, hallo, Peter. **War Ihre Reise nach** Manchester **erfolgreich**?

P. I don't know yet if it was successful, Lucy. But the trip itself was fine.

P. Ich weiß noch nicht, ob sie erfolgreich war, Lucy. Aber die Fahrt selber lief sehr gut.

L. Mr Morgan is waiting for you.

L. Mr Morgan wartet schon auf Sie.

(Peter enters Morgan's office)

(Peter betritt Morgans Büro)

J. Good morning, Peter. How did the trip to Manchester go?

J. Guten Morgen, Peter. Wie lief Ihr Ausflug nach Manchester?

P. I think it's too early to say, Mr Morgan. But the **presentation went well enough** and certainly

P. Ich glaube, es ist noch zu früh, um etwas sagen zu können, Mr Morgan. Aber die **Präsentation ver-**

they showed great interest. As you know, we have some **stiff** competition here.

lief zufriedenstellend und **sie haben großes Interesse gezeigt**. Wie Sie ja wissen, haben wir dort **harte** Konkurrenz.

J. I agree, we can't expect **immediate results** with this assignment. I think we'll have to sit patiently by and just wait for a **decision** ...

J. Das sehe ich auch so, wir können bei diesem Auftrag keine **sofortigen Ergebnisse** erwarten. Ich denke, wir müssen einfach geduldig ausharren und auf eine **Entscheidung** warten ...

Train Yourself

Im letzten Gespräch verwendet James Morgan die Begriffe **»immediate«** und **»immediately«**, **»patient«** und **»patiently«**. »Patient« und »immediate« sind Adjektive, die das Nomen näher bestimmen, »immediately« und »patiently« hingegen sind Adverbien, die das Verb näher bestimmen. **Setzen Sie im folgenden Text entweder das richtige Adverb oder das richtige Adjektiv ein!**

1. Thank you for waiting so *(patient)* for a reply to your letter.
2. I would be grateful for *(immediate)* action in this important matter.
3. We have been *(full)* employed in searching for the causes of the delay.
4. Would you please make sure we are informed *(prompt)*.
5. Our company expects *(complete)* compliance with the terms of the licence agreement.
6. The delay in deliveries cannot *(necessary)* be blamed on our department.
7. Their despatch department is *(usual)* very *(prompt)* in attending to our orders.
8. I am afraid I am not *(complete)* in agreement with your views on this matter.
9. We are happy to report that the performance of the A-300 is *(full)* satisfactory.
10. *(Happy)*, we can report outstanding interim financial results.
11. We would not have waited so *(patient)* if we had known.

12. The Birmingham office is *(unusual)* late in calling back.
13. They complain they were treated very *(bad)* by the new director.
14. *(Bad)* enough, but worse was to follow.

Talk Talk Talk

(James Morgan's office)

(James Morgans Büro)

J. Peter, Melissa might have told you that **an opening** has arisen in the **Marketing Department**, and **we are advertising the post**. I'd like you to take over the **initial selection** process.

J. Peter, Melissa hat Ihnen ja vielleicht schon gesagt, dass sich **eine freie Stelle** in der **Marketing-Abteilung** ergeben hat und wir **für diese Stelle annoncieren**. Ich hätte gerne, dass Sie den **ersten Auswahlprozess** übernehmen.

P. Certainly, but what does that **entail**?

P. Sicher, was **gehört dazu**?

J. First of all, careful reading of the **applications**. With the employment situation as it is, we are expecting quite a number. There are already some on file, so please take those into consideration, too. When you have **sorted out a rough short list of candidates** let's then get together with Melissa and narrow down the selection process.

J. Zunächst einmal das sorgfältige Lesen der **Bewerbungen**. Bei der derzeitigen Situation auf dem Arbeitsmarkt erwarten wir eine ganze Menge davon. Wir haben bereits ein paar Bewerbungen in den Akten, also berücksichtigen Sie diese bitte auch. Wenn Sie **eine erste Auswahl der Bewerber zusammengestellt** haben, schließen Sie sich mit Melissa zusammen und grenzen die Auswahl weiter ein.

P. What should I be looking for?

P. Nach was soll ich denn Ausschau halten?

J. This is a trainee position. We are looking for a young person who

J. Es geht um eine *Trainee*-Position. Wir suchen nach einem

has just completed university or Technical College, preferably with a **degree in economics** or a **business-related discipline**. Melissa will be wanting somebody with marketing potential, with a **forceful personality** – and that sometimes is evident from the first page of a letter of application.

jungen Menschen, der gerade die Universität oder die Technische Hochschule abgeschlossen hat, am besten mit einem Abschluss in **Wirtschaftswissenschaft** oder einem anderen **wirtschaftlichen Ausbildungsfach**. Melissa wird jemanden mit Talent zum Marketing haben wollen, jemanden mit einer **ausgeprägten Persönlichkeit** – und so etwas wird manchmal schon auf der ersten Seite eines Bewerbungsanschreibens ersichtlich.

P. I'm not awfully sure just how forceful Melissa expects a trainee to be!

P. Ich bin mir nicht sicher, wie viel Persönlichkeit Melissa bei einem Trainee wirklich erwartet!

Train Yourself

Suchen Sie in den folgenden Sätzen nach der richtigen Präposition:

1. If you're passing the library on the way to work could you look .... for me and collect anything they have on Adam Smith.
2. Just look .... yourself. You look .... if you've been dragged through a hedge backwards!
3. If you're in the neighbourhood tomorrow look .... and we'll have tea.
4. Could you look this .... in your dictionary for me?
5. They are real snobs. They look .... on anyone they feel is below their own social rank.
6. The problem with kids today is they have nobody to look .... to, that's what my dad says.
7. We'll certainly look .... this matter and see if we can find the cause of the problem.
8. Look ...., there's a car coming for us on the wrong side of the road!
9. Look very carefully .... these notes for me and look .... any mistakes.
10. Look .... you very carefully when you walk through this neighbourhood at night.

Background Information

And **look** here! There are some phrases to note, too!

Look here!	Now just look here, you can't tell me what to do.
Look sharp!	Look sharp, hurry up! Breakfast is in ten minutes!
Look alive!	Get a move on! We haven't got all day, you know!
Look daggers!	He looked daggers at me – he was obviously very annoyed.

Talk Talk Talk

(James Morgan's office)

J. Here are the first applications, Peter. Go through them and make a first selection.

P. Righto (returns to his office). Lucy, be a dear and make me some tea, please. I shall be **tied down** in my office for some time. Now, let's look at these letters ...

(James Morgans Büro)

J. Hier sind die ersten Bewerbungen, Peter. Sehen Sie sie durch und treffen Sie eine Vorauswahl.

P. Klaro (geht in sein Büro zurück). Lucy, seien Sie bitte ein Schatz und kochen Sie mir einen Tee. Ich werde eine Weile in meinem Büro **eingebunden** sein. Gut, dann schauen wir uns mal diese Briefe an ...

Dear Sirs,

Having read your advertisement offering a position in your marketing department, I feel I might be just the person you are looking for. Although I **broke off** my university studies after one semester, I later gathered practical experience in marketing in the shoe department of Holly and Brights, **the big department chain**. After five years in this department, I feel the time has come **to move on to something more demanding**. Possibilities at Holly and Brights are limited, so I am looking for a position in a completely different area of business. I do have some experience of computer technology, having just invested in a PC.

My colleagues at Holly and Bright will testify as to my cheerful and helpful disposition. If you need any further information, please write to me *poste restante* at Herne Bay Post Office because I am in the process of moving address. From July 1, I can be contacted c/o Miss Judy O'Connell, at 35 Cedar Drive, Herne Bay.
Hoping to hear from you soon,

Yours very sincerely,

Bill Boulton

P. Well, I think we can forget that one, for a start. What else is in the post-bag?

P. Tja, ich denke, den können wir schon mal vergessen. Was haben wir denn sonst noch im Postsack?

Dear Mesdames/Sirs,

Further to your advertisement in the Morning Echo, I would like to add my humble name to the list of those you will be interviewing for the vacancy in your marketing department. Perhaps I cannot claim the qualifications required and am a little too advanced in age (52) to hope for a post as trainee, but in my long career with J.P. Engineering I have always been ready to learn something new. You might have read reports that J.P. Engineering is preparing for **retrenchments**, and I feel that for my own security I must begin to look around for alternative employment.
I would therefore be very pleased if you could consider my application for the vacancy in your company. I can promise loyalty, hard work and a willingness to learn new technologies - even those related to the computer age, which I'm afraid has passed me by!

Your loyal and obedient servant,

Henry J. Jobson

Background Information

»Poste restante« (French for »Letters remaining«) describes the department in British Post Offices where letters can be sent and then collected personally by the **addressee**. Addressee? That's the person to whom the letter is sent.
»c/o« is short for »care of«. It is added to the address when the letter is to be delivered into the care of somebody other than the addressee:

Mr John Ripton,
c/o Mrs Jane Simpson,
The Oaks,
Bramley

Do's and Don'ts

»Your loyal and obediant servant«? You will still encounter this archaic way of signing off a formal letter. Variations include: Your loyal and dutiful servant! Charming and genteel as they sound, resist any temptation to use them!

Train Yourself

Let's take a break ...

»Break« als Verb oder Nomen ist oft in umgangssprachlichen Ausdrücken zu finden. **Setzen Sie in den folgenden Sätzen die passende Form ein:**

1. I'm tired. Let's take a ______.
2. Jim and Jane aren't going out together any more. They ______ off.
3. Police are investigating a ______ at the local bank.
4. Police were called in to ______ the demonstration.
5. I'll have to get a new car. Mine is constantly ______.

6. The right wing of the party ________ from the mainstream.
7. The ship was ________ for scrap.
8. An epidemic of measles has ________ in the north of the country.

Talk Talk Talk

(Peter's office. James Morgan enters)	(Peters Büro. James Morgan tritt ein)
J. So how's it going, Peter? Have you found our ideal candidate yet?	J. Wie läuft es, Peter? Haben Sie schon unseren Traumkandidaten gefunden?
P. I've only been through two letters so far, and they certainly don't qualify.	P. Ich habe bis jetzt erst zwei Briefe durch und sie haben sich beide ganz sicher nicht qualifiziert.
J. Mind if I look?	J. Was dagegen, wenn ich mal einen Blick darauf werfe?
P. Not at all, help yourself!	P. Überhaupt nicht, nur zu!
(James Morgan reads the letters)	(James Morgan liest die Briefe)
J. You know what dismays me, Peter? Some people seem incapable of reading an advertisement correctly. We were very clear indeed in stating our **requirements**. I just can't see how anybody could fail to understand. I'm just unable to explain it.	J. Wissen Sie, was ich wirklich erschreckend finde, Peter? Einige Leute scheinen nicht in der Lage zu sein, eine Anzeige korrekt zu lesen. Wir haben unsere **Anforderungen** klar ausgedrückt. Es ist mir schleierhaft, wie jemand sie missverstehen kann. Ich kann so etwas einfach nicht erklären.
P. I think the letters were written from a position of despair. Boulton is obviously bored with his depart-	P. Ich denke, diese Briefe wurden aus der Verzweiflung heraus geschrieben. Boulton ist in seinem

ment store job, and Jobson fears he'll be out of a job before long.

Kaufhaus-Job offensichtlich gelangweilt und Jobson fürchtet, dass er bald ohne Job dastehen wird.

J. But that's no reason to regard us as an escape route ...

J. Aber das ist noch kein Grund, uns als letzten Ausweg zu missbrauchen ...

Train Yourself

»Incapable« oder **»unable«**? Beide Wörter bedeuten im Englischen, dass man nicht in der Lage ist, etwas zu tun, obwohl »incapable« eine eher negative Bedeutung hat und mit »unfähig« übersetzt wird. »He is quite incapable of assuming the position of Managing Director« (Das soll heißen, dass er nicht die Fähigkeiten besitzt, Geschäftsführer zu werden). »Is she totally incapable of doing that job properly?«. »Incapable« verwendet man mit »of« und der Gerundform des Verbs; »unable« verlangt einen Infinitiv. **Und nun sollten Sie dazu in der Lage sein, die folgenden Sätze zu vervollständigen!**

1. I regret we are unable *(accept)* your kind invitation to dinner.
2. She is totally incapable *(tell)* him that she wants a divorce.
3. Are you incapable *(read)* the small print on the sales agreement?
4. I am afraid we are unable *(deliver)* by the date you mention.
5. He appears to be incapable *(be)* on time for any appointment.
6. I must confess I am unable *(see)* the purpose of your company's proposal.
7. That company appears incapable *(pay)* its debts on time.
8. I am very sorry I was unable *(make)* the appointment.

Talk Talk Talk

P. Do we have a **regular form of letter to reply to unsuccessful applicants**?

P. Haben wir ein **standardisiertes Absageschreiben für abgelehnte Kandidaten**?

J. Yes, Lucy can help you there. But in the case of these two appli-

J. Ja, Lucy kann Ihnen da helfen. Aber ich denke, im Fall dieser

cants I think a personal letter might be kinder. See what you can do!

beiden Bewerber wäre ein persönlicher Brief freundlicher. Schauen Sie doch mal, was Sie machen können!

P. I'll do my best but I don't have much experience of this sort of thing ...

P. Ich versuche mein Bestes, aber ich habe nicht viel Erfahrung in solchen Dingen ...

Dear Mr Boulton,

Thank you for your letter responding to our advertisement in the Morning Echo. **I regret to inform you that your impressive professional experience does not completely match the requirements of the position we are seeking to fill.**
Thank you, nonetheless, for your interest, and wishing you every success in your present career.

Yours sincerely,

Peter Brückner,
Assistant Managing Director

Talk Talk Talk

(James Morgan's office. Peter enters)

(James Morgans Büro. Peter tritt ein)

P. Do you think this reply will do?

P. Glauben Sie, dass diese Antwort angemessen ist?

J. (reads it) I think that's very **well worded**. I don't see the point of being too **offhand**. A personal touch can't do any harm. You can

J. (liest den Brief) Ich finde, er ist sehr gut **formuliert**. Ich sehe keinen Grund dafür, zu **unpersönlich** zu sein. Ein persönlicher

use the same wording in the second letter.

Touch kann nichts schaden. Sie können dieselbe Formulierung beim zweiten Brief verwenden.

P. I'll give them to Lucy to type and then get **stuck into** the others ...

P. Ich werde sie Lucy zum Abtippen geben und mich dann in die anderen **vertiefen** ...

Train Yourself

Ein Lebenslauf ist einer der wichtigsten Teile einer Bewerbung. Der englische Begriff dafür, »CV«, steht kurz für den lateinischen Ausdruck »Curriculum Vitae«. **Suchen Sie im folgenden Lebenslauf die fehlenden Verben und setzen Sie sie in die korrekte Zeit!**

Name: John Tatterell
I ______ in Plymouth, Devon, on May 22, 1968. After ______ Plymouth Grammar School for six years, I ______ with A-Level passes in English, French and Social Studies. I ______ one year off and ______ extensively in North and South America. On ______ to Britain in 1987, I ______ for a course in business studies at Hendon Technical College. After ______ the course in 1989, I ______ Jackson and Tucker Limited as a management trainee. During my time there, I ______ experience in all departments of the company and at present I ______ as assistant to the Marketing Director. My French ______ still fluent, and I ______ German and Spanish during my spare time. My duties at Jackson and Tucker ______ contacts with foreign clients and ______ participation in trade fairs in mainland Europe. This work ______ me to Milan, Munich, Stockholm and Copenhagen, and I ______ very much at home in an international arena.

return, organise, gain, take, join, leave, employ, enrol, feel, be, attend, complete, include, study, be born, travel, maintain.

(Peter reads the next letter)

(Peter liest den nächsten Brief)

Dear Sirs/Mesdames,

I would be grateful if you considered my application for the position your company has advertised in the Morning Echo. As you will see from the **accompanying CV**, I have just left university with a Master's degree in Business Administration and am looking for a post which would allow me to **put into practice** what I have learnt over the past five years. With my background in computer studies, a company such as yours would offer the ideal opportunity for me. One year of my degree course was **devoted to** marketing and market research, and **I would be very happy to have the chance to work in the kind of area your advertisement describes**. I am available under the above address and telephone number to provide additional information, and of course I am available at any time to attend a personal interview.

Yours faithfully,

Roger Fenton

Talk Talk Talk

(James Morgan's office)

(James Morgans Büro)

P. Mr Morgan, this letter here sounds promising.

P. Mr Morgan, dieser Brief hier klingt viel versprechend.

J. Let's have a look! (He reads the letter). You're right. The young man seems to have the qualifications we are looking for. **Some practical experience** would have been desirable, but he would certainly get that here. Where's his CV?

J. Schauen wir mal! (Er liest den Brief) Sie haben Recht. Dieser junge Mann scheint genau die Qualifikationen zu haben, die wir suchen. Ein paar **praktische Erfahrungen** wären zwar wünschenswert gewesen, aber die wird er hier schon noch bekommen. Wo ist sein Lebenslauf?

CV - Roger Fenton.

Born: February 20, 1975, in Carlisle.
Education:
Primary: St. Christopher's Preparatory School, Carlisle.
Secondary: Carlisle Grammar School.
Certificates: 6 GSCEs (English Language, English Literature, History, Biology, Economics, French). 3 A-Levels: (English, Economics, Business Studies).
Universities: University of York. BA (Economics, American Studies); London School of Economics (MBA).
Additional studies and work experience: One year (1998-99) exchange student at Yale University, U.S.A. Six months (1995) practical experience in the Marketing Division of Santos Holdings, London.
References can be obtained from Professor Hamilton Harding of the University of York and Dr. Jonathan Digby-Smith, Managing Director, Santos Holdings.

Talk Talk Talk

J. Quite impressive. Reads well, even though I do prefer a **written CV** instead of one in this **tabular form**. It makes it more difficult to assess the person behind the facts. But, of course, we'll be inviting him for an interview. Young Fenton certainly **falls into** the short-list category. You'll have **made up a file** already, Peter?

J. Recht eindrucksvoll. Liest sich sehr gut, obwohl ich einen **ausformulierten Lebenslauf** einem in dieser **tabellarischen Form** vorziehe. So ist es schwieriger, den Mensch hinter den Daten einzuschätzen. Aber natürlich werden wir ihn zu einem Gespräch einladen. Unser junger Mr Fenton **fällt** ganz sicher **in** die Vorauswahl. Haben Sie bereits **einen Ordner angelegt**, Peter?

P. Well, this is the first application that qualifies, so I'll create a file right now and put the letter in it.

P. Na ja, das ist die erste Bewerbung, die sich qualifiziert, also werde ich sofort einen Ordner

What about a reply to the application?

anlegen und den Brief einfügen. Wie sieht es mit einer Antwort auf die Bewerbung aus?

J. I think we can send out a standard reply to applicants we shall be inviting for an interview. I'll leave that to you ...

J. Ich denke, wir können an die Bewerber, die wir zu einem Gespräch einladen, einen Standardbrief schicken. Das überlasse ich Ihnen ...

Train Yourself

Impression, impressive, impressively, to impress? **Finden Sie die richtige Form (inklusive Präposition) für die folgenden Sätze:**

1. I was very ______ his performance.
2. I didn't find his performance as ______ as the last time I saw him in the concert hall.
3. The new system has been functioning most ______ since its installation.
4. What kind of ______ did she leave ______ you?
5. That's a very ______ motorbike you've got there.
6. Were you really ______ what she said?
7. I find it very difficult ______ him with the facts.
8. Did you think our presentation left ______ the audience?
9. I thought he spoke ______ about a difficult subject.
10. They said they were very ______ what he had to say.

(Peter dictates ...)

(Peter diktiert ...)

Dear Mr Fenton,

We acknowledge receipt of your application for the position which has become available in our Marketing Department, and **we have pleasure in inviting you for an interview**, at a date yet to be set. Interviews will, however, be held during the last two weeks of July. If for any reason you are unable to come to London during this time, please let us know in good time and we shall endeavour to organise our schedule to match yours.

Yours sincerely,

Peter Brückner,
Assistant Managing Director

(Peter opens another letter) (Peter öffnet einen weiteren Brief)

Dear Sirs,

My attention was caught by your company's insertion in the Morning Echo, advertising the vacancy in your Marketing Department. **I would be very grateful if you considered my application for the post.** For the past three years I have been employed by the Robinson public relations agency, mostly writing advertising copy (cf. accompanying CV). I would now like very much to make the change to the purely business sector and, in particular, the hi-tech field. For that reason, I would be very interested indeed in working for a company such as yours.
Hoping to hear from you soon,

Yours faithfully,

Nigel Branson

Nigel Branson's CV:

Nigel John Branson.

Born October 12, 1975, in Huddersfield, Yorkshire. Educated at St. Christopher's Preparators School and Huddersfield Grammar School, leaving in 1993 with 7 GSCEs and 3 A-Levels (English, History and Geography). Four years study (1993-97) at the University of Sussex, Brighton, graduating with BA (2/1 grade). In September, 1997, joined Robinson Public Relations, London, as copy-writer.

Background information

The word **»acknowledge«** has several meanings in the business English vocabulary. In the above letter, it is used to register receipt of the job application – »We acknowledge receipt of your letter of ...«. In business letters it is a common substitute for: »Thank you for your letter of ...«

Other uses are seen in the following examples:

1. We acknowledge your company's complaints and will do all we can to rectify the situation (agree to the truth of).
2. The lawyers acknowledged the deed and added it to the file (gave it legal validity, accepted it as valid).
3. The accountant acknowledged his responsibility for the mistake in the annual report (admitted his guilt).
4. We acknowledge your efforts to correct the mistake (we express appreciation).
5. They acknowledged our presence at the concert (took notice of).
6. We acknowledge Mr Hoskins as the responsible officer in this case (recognise his authority).

The abbreviations **c.f.** and **cf.** have very different meanings in business English:
1. c.f. – »carried forward« – used in financial statements when a sum or figure is »carried forward« from one column or page to another.
2. cf – (as used in the above letter) »compare« (from the Latin imperative *confer* – compare). In Nigel Branson's letter, he uses the abbreviation to draw attention to the fact that his summarised career is dealt with in more detail in an accompanying CV.

Train Yourself

Das Wort »acknowledge« hat viele Synonyme, z. B.: *accept, admit, allow, avow, certify, concede, confess, confirm, grant, own, profess, recognise.*

Finden Sie in den folgenden Sätzen die korrekten Synonyme für dieses Wort!

1. Could your lawyer please acknowledge the validity of the will?
2. I acknowledge total responsibility for the errors in the report.
3. We acknowledge receipt of your letter of March 12.
4. The company acknowledged our authority to act in this matter.
5. He acknowledged our presence at the meeting but still ignored us.
6. The board acknowledged him as the best person to represent the company.
7. When finally charged with embezzlement, he acknowledged his guilt.
8. They acknowledged their admiration for the company's recovery.

Talk Talk Talk

(Peter's Office. Melissa enters)	(Peters Büro. Melissa tritt ein)
M. Hope I'm not disturbing, but I was just passing the door and curiosity **got the better of** me. Have you found anyone promising?	M. Ich hoffe, ich störe nicht, aber ich kam gerade an Ihrer Tür vorbei und **konnte der Neugier nicht widerstehen**. Haben Sie schon jemand Vielversprechenden entdeckt?
P. Well, yes and no – at least we've got the start of a short-list of candidates. When are you joining the selection panel?	P. Tja, ja und nein – wenigstens konnten wir schon eine Vorauswahl-Liste anlegen. Wann werden Sie zur Bewerberauswahl dazukommen?
M. I'll be there at the interviews. I'm leaving the hard work to you. But there are rewards – come on, it's my round at the *Nag's Head* ...	M. Ich werde bei den Vorstellungsgesprächen dabei sein. Ich überlasse Ihnen die Knochenarbeit. Aber Sie sollen auch belohnt werden – kommen Sie, ich spendiere eine Runde im *Nag's Head* ...
(The *Nag's Head pub*)	(Im *Nag's Head Pub*)

M. Cheers, Peter! How many possibles have you got so far?

M. Prost, Peter! Wie viele mögliche Kandidaten haben Sie bis jetzt?

P. Just two, really, although a couple more are on file. They **wrote inquiring** about employment possibilities before we inserted the advertisement.

P. Erst zwei, obwohl wir noch ein paar in den Akten haben. Sie haben **Initiativbewerbungen** an uns geschickt, bevor wir die Stellenanzeige aufgegeben hatten.

M. And how many more applications have you got to read?

M. Und wie viele Bewerbungen müssen Sie noch lesen?

P. About half a dozen, I believe. James wants to **narrow** the shortlist **down** to no more than six, anyway.

P. Etwa ein halbes Dutzend, schätze ich. James möchte die Vorauswahl-Liste auf nicht mehr als sechs Bewerber **einschränken**.

M. Well, **keep me posted –** I'll be working with whomever is chosen for the job.

M. Na gut, **halten Sie mich auf dem Laufenden –** ich werde schließlich mit dem ausgewählten Bewerber zusammenarbeiten.

P. Don't worry – you can take over the selection process right now, if you want.

P. Keine Sorge – Sie können das Auswahlverfahren sofort übernehmen, wenn Sie wollen.

M. No thanks, Peter – that's your job!

M. Nein, vielen Dank, Peter – das ist Ihr Job!

Train Yourself

Who, whom oder *whose*?

Füllen Sie die Lücken mit der korrekten Form!

1. With ________ were you talking so long on the telephone?
2. To ________ address did you send that letter?
3. ________ did you talk to for so long on the phone last night?
4. Have you yet decided ________ should head the company next year?

5. I never realised __________ she really was.
6. __________ would you like to accompany you to the dinner?
7. __________ name is to appear at the top of the letter?
8. By __________ did you say that book is written?
9. You never told me __________ actually performed the part.
10. On __________ shoulders will the blame ultimately rest?

Talk Talk Talk

(Peter's office. Steve enters)	(Peters Büro. Steve tritt ein)
S. Hi, Peter! Are you still **head-hunting**?	S. Hi, Peter! Immer noch beim **»Head-hunting«**?
P. Hi, Steve! I haven't seen you for a while. Have you been **off-base**?	P. Hi, Steve! Lange nicht gesehen. Waren Sie **außerhalb** unterwegs?
S. I had to do the usual round of the sales posts. One of the guys had heard there was a place in marketing. He wants out of sales and would be interested in something else within the company. I told him to get an application in.	S. Ich habe die übliche Tour bei unseren Verkaufsstellen gemacht. Einer von den Kollegen hat gehört, dass es eine Stelle im Marketing gibt. Er möchte aus dem Verkauf heraus und ist an einer Anstellung in der Firma selbst interessiert. Ich habe ihm gesagt, er soll eine Bewerbung einreichen.
P. I'm working through them right now. But this position is for a young career-starter, you know.	P. Ich arbeite mich gerade durch. Aber diese Position ist für einen jungen Berufseinsteiger gedacht, wissen Sie.
S. Never too late to start, Peter old chap!	S. Es ist nie zu spät einzusteigen, Peter, alter Freund!

Background Information

Head-hunting

In this highly competitive professional world, more and more companies are engaging specialist firms to hunt specifically for the employees they need. The practice is called »head-hunting«.

Train Yourself

Interest, interested, interesting ...

Vervollständigen Sie die folgenden Sätze mit den passenden Wörtern (und den Präpositionen, wenn möglich)!

1. The company found this proposal __________ particular __________ .
2. The company found this proposal particularly __________ .
3. The company is particularly __________ this proposal.
4. The company's __________ has been caught __________ the proposal.
5. She made an __________ impression on us.
6. Would a brochure __________ your company?
7. Would a brochure be of __________ your company?
8. They sat through the whole lecture. They were very __________ .
9. They sat through the whole lecture. They found it very __________ .
10. Are you really __________ what he has to say?
11. The suggestion aroused much __________ .
12. The audience found the suggestion very __________ .

Talk Talk Talk

(Peter's office. Peter takes a fax from the machine)

(Peters Büro. Peter nimmt ein Fax aus dem Gerät)

P. Well, Steve's man lost no time ...

P. Na so was, Steves Spezi hat keine Zeit verloren ...

Dear Mr Brückner,

Mr Blackman informs me that a position has become vacant in ERGO's Marketing Department, and I would be grateful if you were able to consider my application. Although I have been employed in sales for ERGO for the past five years I feel that in that time I have acquired skills which could benefit the company in a wider area. After five years in sales, I must confess that I would like to move on and gain further experience within the company.
My full details and work record are, of course, on file, so I shan't bother you with a CV, **but if you require any further information I am only too ready to supply it**.
Hoping for a favourable response,

Yours sincerely,

Dale Spinks

Background Information

The expression **»only too«** is found frequently in business correspondence. It is a slightly archaic form, which can just as easily – only too easily – be substituted by »very«:

a) I shall be only too (very) pleased to comply with your wishes.
b) We shall be only too (very) ready for your comments.
c) We shall be only too (very) delighted to see you next Tuesday.
d) They were only too (very) glad to see the company fail.
e) He was only too (very) glad to call off the meeting.

Train Yourself

Vervollständigen Sie folgende Sätze mit »only« oder »only too«:

1. I wanted to meet her before she left. Now it's too late.
2. They should be pleased they didn't take up that offer.

3. I'm grateful for the help you gave me.
4. It's not the anger it causes, but also the pain.
5. We've two miles to go before we get home.
6. I shall be glad to do that for you.

Talk Talk Talk

(Peter's Office. Chip, the courier-messenger, enters)

(Peters Büro. Chip, der Kurierbote, tritt ein)

P. Hello, Chip! What can I do for you?

P. Hallo, Chip! Was kann ich für dich tun?

C. This package from Dickens and Jolly is for you – they asked me to deliver it personally. Oh, Mr Brückner, I hear there's a vacancy in the Marketing Department.

C. Dieses Paket ist für Sie, von Dickens und Jolly – sie haben mich gebeten, es persönlich abzugeben. Oh, Mr Brückner, ich habe gehört, dass es eine freie Stelle in der Marketing-Abteilung gibt.

P. Oh, no, Chip, not you, too!

P. Oh, nein, Chip, nicht du auch noch!

C. Good lord, you wouldn't catch me wanting to work in there **for all the tea in China**! I like my freedom, **buzzing about** the place on a motorbike is my idea of a job. I wouldn't last a morning in an office with Miss Walker. That miss and me would be a real mistake!

C. Um Himmels Willen, **nicht für alles Geld der Welt** möchte ich hier arbeiten! Ich mag meine Freiheit und mit dem Motorrad **herumzufahren** ist meine Vorstellung von einem Traumjob. Ich würde es keinen Vormittag zusammen in einem Büro mit Miss Walker aushalten. Diese Dame und ich – das würde nicht gut gehen!

P. Chip, if you were as fast on your motorbike as you are with words

P. Chip, wenn du mit deinem Motorrad so schnell wärst wie mit

we'd have the most efficient courier service in London. But just watch what you have to say about Miss Walker, you mischievous miscreant!

deinem Mundwerk, wärst du der effektivste Kurierfahrer in London. Aber sei vorsichtig, was du über Miss Walker sagst, du schändliches Schandmaul!

C. Hey, you're not so bad with the words yourself! At least, for a German!

C. Hey, Sie können aber auch gut mit Worten umgehen! Wenigstens für einen Deutschen!

P. Out with you, before I find a missile to chuck at you ...

P. Raus mit dir, bevor ich etwas finde, dass ich nach dir werfen kann ...

Train Yourself

Finden Sie die passenden Wörter zu den Umschreibungen.
Sie fangen alle mit der Vorsilbe »mis-« an, also keine »Missgriffe« bitte!

1. Do this and you pronounce a word incorrectly. ....
2. Bad luck strikes you if you experience this. ....
3. This person doesn't like people and avoids society. ....
4. If you shape or form something badly it will be ... .
5. Give out money wastefully and you ... .
6. A mixture or medley of anything. ....
7. Give somebody the wrong instructions or advice and you... ....
8. A feeling of mistrust or apprehension. ....
9. Somebody who just doesn't belong in a particular place or environment. ....
10. A crime or evil act. ....
11. Bad behaviour. ....
12. Use the wrong name or word and you're guilty of a... ....

misspend, misnomer, miscellany, misanthrope, mischance, misfit, misdeed, misconduct, misgiving, mispronounce, misshapen, misdirect.

Vocabulary

addressee	Adressat
to advertise a post	eine Stelle annoncieren
to break off	aufhören/abbrechen
(a) business-related discipline	wirtschaftliches Ausbildungsfach
to buzz about	umhersausen
a degree in economics	Abschluss in Wirtschaftswissenschaft
devoted to	gewidmet
discipline	hier: Fachgebiet
to entail	beinhalten/nach sich ziehen
to fall into	hineinfallen (im Sinne von »dazu gehören«) (Redewendung)
for all the tea in China	etwa: Für alles Geld der Welt
forceful	hier: ausgeprägt (Charakter)
to get the better of	etwas nachgeben, nicht widerstehen können
initial	anfänglich
to keep sb. posted	auf dem Laufenden halten/ informieren
to make up a file	einen Ordner anlegen
to narrow down	eingrenzen
off-base	außerhalb (einer Firma etc.)
offhand	unpersönlich
(an) opening	eine freie Stelle
requirements	Anforderungen
to put into practice	in die Praxis umsetzen
retrenchment	Einschränkung/Kürzung; Kostenreduzierung
to sort out	aussortieren
stiff	steif/hier: rauh, umkämpft
to stuck into sth.	sich in etwas vertiefen/ «hineinknien«
tabular	tabellarisch
(to be) tied down	in etwas eingebunden sein
well-worded	wohl formuliert

Letter of reply
Antwortschreiben

Here we go

Viele Bewerbungen für die freie Stelle in der Marketingabteilung sind bei ERGO Limited eingegangen. Doch Dank Peters Hilfe konnten die vielversprechendsten Bewerber ausgemacht werden. Aber die Entscheidung fällt nicht leicht. Peter kann einen guten Vorschlag einbringen, der letztlich zum lang erwarteten Ergebnis führt, und dieses Ergebnis ist gleichzeitig noch für eine freudige Überraschung gut ...

Talk Talk Talk

(The front office of ERGO Limited. Peter enters)	(Das Eingangsbüro von ERGO Limited. Peter tritt ein)
L. Good morning, Peter! Did you have a good weekend?	L. Guten Morgen, Peter! Hatten Sie ein schönes Wochenende?
P. I visited my friends in Sussex. They took me hunting. What strange sports you English have!	P. Ich habe meine Freunde in Sussex besucht. Sie haben mich zur Jagd mitgenommen. Ihr Engländer habt schon seltsame Sportarten!
L. You actually rode in the hunt?	L. Sind Sie tatsächlich bei der Jagd mitgeritten?
P. I rode in a motor-car! I let the others risk their necks. And they were incapable of finding one single fox!	P. Ich bin im Auto gefahren! Sollen die anderen ihren Hals riskieren. Die haben es nicht mal geschafft, einen einzigen Fuchs aufzuspüren!

J. Good morning, Peter – did I hear right? You went hunting? You insensitive chap! That's a very controversial way for a visitor to England to spend his weekends!

J. Guten Morgen, Peter – habe ich da richtig gehört? Sie waren auf einer Jagd? Sie unempfindsamer Kerl! Das ist schon eine sehr umstrittene Art und Weise für einen England-Besucher, seine Wochenenden zu verbringen!

L. Oh, don't you listen to Mr Morgan, Peter! He says golf is his sport, but I know for a fact that sometimes he goes shooting in Scotland!

L. Ach was, hören Sie nicht auf Mr Morgan, Peter! Er behauptet ja, Golf wäre seine Sportart, aber ich weiß ganz genau, dass er manchmal zum Schießen nach Schottland fährt!

J. Wrong again, Lucy. I only visit Scotland for the whisky. Talking of which, you can add a dash to my morning tea ...

J. Schon wieder falsch! Ich besuche Schottland nur wegen des Whiskys. Da wir gerade davon sprechen, Sie können mir einen Schuss davon in meinen Frühstückstee gießen ...

Train Yourself

Wie lassen sich die Sätze durch die Vorsilben ab-, dis-, il-, im-, in-, un- verneinen?

1. She loves animals. She's ______ capable of killing a fly.
2. He's so obstinate. He's quite ______ pervious to any reasonable argument.
3. I'm away on business on that day, so I am ______ able to accept the invitation.
4. The bill is much too high for the amount of work involved. It's ______ proportionate.
5. I've never before seen them behave like that. It's quite ______ normal.
6. The company gave him one month's notice – how ______ sensitive.
7. He took the news without displaying any emotion, ______ passively.

8. Despite the company's poor performance, the share price remained ______ affected.
9. I wouldn't invest at this time, if I were you - the stock market seems very ______ stable.
10. The contract is for three months only because the position is ______ secure.
11. He was summarily sacked because of ______ seemly behaviour.
12. The company could have kept him until the end of the month. I thought its treatment of him was quite ______ gracious.
13. I can't read the letter - his handwriting is ______ legible.
14. They allow smoking in the office. It's a very ______ healthy environment.
15. I'll have to leave. The working atmosphere is quite ______ tolerable.
16. He was very ______ certain, unable to choose which course to follow.

Talk Talk Talk

(Peter's office. James Morgan enters)	(Peters Büro. James Morgen tritt ein)
J. How far are you with the job applications, Peter?	J. Wie weit sind Sie mit den Bewerbungen, Peter?
P. Just two to go, unless any more arrive.	P. Es sind nur noch zwei zu erledigen, falls nicht noch mehr kommen.
J. We'll have **to close the shortlist** this week. We've still got the interviews to organise.	J. Wir müssen die **Vorauswahl** noch diese Woche **abschließen**. Die Interviews müssen wir auch noch organisieren.
P. At least one of the remaining letters looks quite promising, what do you think?	P. Zumindest einer der übrigen Briefe sieht viel versprechend aus, was meinen Sie?

Dear Sirs/Mesdames,

In response to your company's advertisement in the Morning Echo, I would like to apply for the vacant post. I have just graduated with a Master's Degree in Business Administration from the University of Essex and I am actively looking for a position in the Marketing Department of a company such as yours. I have practical experience of marketing, gathered during one year's job-training in the United States, where I worked in the Marketing Division of Johnson and Sears, one of the country's largest public relations companies. I attach a full CV, with references, and would be very happy to respond to any questions you may have.

Yours faithfully,

John Smith-Powell

P. But, **by way of contrast**, just look at this letter!

P. Schauen Sie sich **als Gegenbeispiel** mal diesen Brief an!

Dear Sir/Madam,

Look no further. I am the man you want for the job you advertised in the Morning Echo. You won't find a better man for the position, or anyone more loyal. My marketing experience knows practically no boundaries – for the past three years I have been street-selling time-share deals, with great success. Just ask my employers – or my former employers, because their company has just been closed down, allegedly for illicit trading after a dissatisfied salesman blew the whistle. Hence, I'm available immediately. Please give me a call at the above number if you're interested – and interested you must be!

Yours in great expectation,

Thomas (Tom) Fosters

J. I don't believe it! We should frame that one, as an example of how *not* to get a job!

J. Das fasse ich ja nicht! Den sollten wir einrahmen als Beispiel dafür, wie man einen Job *nicht* bekommt.

P. But how do we reply to it?

P. Aber wie antworten wir darauf?

J. It doesn't really merit a reply. Or send the briefest of acknowledgements. Just one question, have you checked the email in-basket today?

J. Eigentlich verdient er gar keine Antwort. Oder schicken Sie ihm die kürzeste, die es nur gibt! Nur eine Frage, haben Sie heute schon in den E-Mail-Posteingang geschaut?

P. I've been so busy that I haven't got around to it. But I'll do it right away.

P. Ich war so beschäftigt, dass ich nicht dazu gekommen bin, aber das mache ich jetzt gleich.

Do's and Don'ts

If you are writing a **job application** in English, don't be misled by your experience of English casualness and humour. In dealings as important as this, the British are as serious as the Germans. So abandon any idea of catching a prospective employer's attention with a »I am the person you're looking for« approach. Your application can be just as eye-catching if it is succinctly and correctly written.

Train Yourself

Verbinden Sie in den folgenden Sätzen das Verb »to get« mit der jeweils passenden Präposition:

1. She'll get _______ quite easily on that salary.
2. He is an impressive young man and will certainly get _______ in life.
3. If you live beyond your means you'll soon get _______ debt.
4. They want to get _______ on the deal as quickly as possible.
5. So what are you getting _______ to these days?

6. Get ________ it! You have to keep up with the times!
7. Are we all here? Right, let's get ________ to business.
8. The boss is fine. You'll have no problem getting ________ with him.
9. Can you get ________ the 1999 file for me please, Lucy!
10. I don't think he'll ever get ________ the death of his wife.
11. The songs from that new musical really get ________ your skin.
12. The new board chairman will find it difficult to get his views ________.

across, along, by, down, in, into, on, out, over, under, up, with.

Talk Talk Talk

(Peter's office.
James Morgan enters)

(Peters Büro.
James Morgan tritt ein)

J. I don't want to rush you, Peter, but do you have any more applications to **shift through.**

J. Peter, ich will Sie nicht hetzen, aber haben Sie noch mehr Bewerbungen **durchzuschauen**?

P. No, I've gone through them all now and **whittled** them **down** to a **short-list** of seven. Here they are.

P. Nein, ich bin sie alle durchgegangen und habe sie auf eine **Auswahlliste** von sieben **reduziert**. Hier sind sie.

J. Fine, I didn't really expect you to get through them that quickly. This afternoon we'll have a meeting with Melissa and prepare the interviews. We can send out a **form-letter** inviting the short-listed candidates to an interview. I'll leave you to **draft** it …

J. Gut, ich hatte wirklich nicht erwartet, dass Sie so schnell damit fertig werden. Heute Nachmittag werden wir uns mit Melissa treffen und die Bewerbungsgespräche vorbereiten. Wir können den vorausgewählten Kandidaten einen **Formbrief** schicken, um sie zum Gespräch einzuladen. Sie können ihn **entwerfen** …

(Peter writes …)

(Peter schreibt …)

Dear ...

Following your application for the position of Assistant Marketing Officer at ERGO Limited headquarters here in London, **we have pleasure in inviting you** to an interview next week. Interviews are being held on Tuesday and Wednesday, August 14-15, between 9 AM and 3 PM. Would you please call our secretary, Ms Lucy Sparrow, to arrange a convenient day and time.

We look forward very much to meeting you and wish you every success with your application.

Yours sincerely,

Peter Brückner,
Assistant Managing Director

Train Yourself

Haben Sie die erste Übung mit »to get« vervollständigt? **Dann versuchen Sie sich jetzt an dieser Fortsetzung!**

1. The company made good progress and rapidly got ______ .
2. He got ______ that tricky situation without much difficulty.
3. He is always getting ______ trouble.
4. If I can find the time, I'll get ______ to it.
5. Considering the seriousness of the crime, he got ______ lightly.
6. The company soon went bankrupt. It got ______ an enormous amount of money in no time at all.
7. Your company's sales people are on the road a lot. They certainly get ______ .
8. Can you get ______ those documents without attracting attention?
9. It's difficult to understand at first, but persist and you'll get ______ .
10. She's in a very strange mood. What can have got ______ her?
11. Grab a pen and get this ______ in writing.
12. He got ______ the boss by waiting until the last moment before handing in his notice.

13. Get all the letters ______ and let's make a short-list.
14. He got ______ that problem by just ignoring it.

around, at, back, down, into, off, through, on, out, round to, there, together.

Talk Talk Talk

(Peter enters office, Lucy greets him)	(Peter betritt das Büro, Lucy begrüßt ihn)
L. Good morning, Peter. Do you have a lot of work to do this morning?	L. Guten Morgen, Peter. Haben Sie heute Morgen viel zu tun?
P. Oh, the usual, Lucy. Why?	P. Ach, das Übliche, Lucy. Warum?
L. Oh, you'll soon see why!	L. Sie werden gleich sehen, warum!
(James Morgan enters)	(James Morgan kommt herein)
J. Well, Lucy, where is it?	J. Lucy, wo ist es?
L. Still on ice. I was waiting for Mr Brückner to arrive.	L. Noch auf Eis. Ich habe auf Mr Brückner gewartet.
J. Can't get started without him, can we. Right, Lucy, serve up!	J. Ohne ihn können wir nicht anfangen, nicht wahr. Gut, Lucy, servieren Sie.
P. Champagne again? Somebody's birthday?	P. Schon wieder Champagner? Hat jemand Geburtstag?
(Melissa and Beryl both enter)	(Melissa und Beryl kommen herein)
M. Not ours, anyway.	M. Wir jedenfalls nicht.

J. Peter, you're to blame. Keep this up and our champagne bill alone will **sink** the company.

J. Peter, Sie sind schuld. Machen Sie weiter so und unsere Champagnerrechnung wird die Firma **ruinieren**.

P. Me?

P. Ich?

J. You secured the Newcom Technology franchise, dear chap! Another coup for you – I'm beginning to worry about the security of my position here!

J. Sie haben uns den Newcom Technology-Franchise gesichert, mein Guter! Schon wieder ein Streich für Sie – ich fange an, mir Sorgen um die Sicherheit meiner Position hier zu machen!

P. The Newcom franchise. Good heavens! I'd forgotten all about it.

P. Die Newcom-Franchise. Gütiger Himmel! Das hatte ich schon ganz vergessen.

J. Well, Newcom hadn't. This letter came today – but first a glass of bubbly and then you and I are off for a celebration lunch ...

J. Nun, Newcom nicht. Dieser Brief kam heute an – aber erst ein Glas Champus und dann machen wir beide uns auf den Weg zu einem festlichen Mittagessen ...

(Peter reads the letter ...)

(Peter liest den Brief ...)

Mr James Morgan,

Managing Director,
ERGO Limited

Dear Mr Morgan,

Following our very fruitful discussions with Mr Peter Brückner, your Assistant Managing Director, and consultations with our lawyers, we are pleased to inform you that we have decided to grant ERGO Limited the franchise for the distribution and marketing of our new product, »Instantweb«, in the United States. Mr Brückner presented a very

convincing argument in favour of ERGO, stressing the depth and breadth of the company's American experience and involvement.
We would like to propose a further meeting now between senior management representatives and lawyers representing both companies to complete the franchise formalities and draw up the relevant agreement and documentation. We would obviously be very happy to see Mr Brückner again as a member of your team.
In anticipation of a very successful co-operation,
I remain,
Yours sincerely,

Joshua Streatham,
Managing Director,
Newcom Technologies

Talk Talk Talk

J. Well, there you have it in **black and white**, Peter. Congratulations! You obviously made a big impression in Manchester.

J. Nun, hier haben Sie es **schwarz auf weiß**, Peter. Gratuliere! Sie haben offensichtlich in Manchester großen Eindruck gemacht.

M. Yes, here's to you Peter – you're becoming quite indispensable ...

M. Ja, auf Sie, Peter – Sie werden hier ziemlich unentbehrlich ...

Background Information

The word **»fruit«** has **»given fruit«** to various expressive words and expressions in English ...

Fruitful meaning productive, beneficial. The board meeting was very fruitful.

Fruitless meaning the opposite. Their search for the cause of the problem remained fruitless.

Fruition meaning the enjoyment or attainment of something desired. He lived to see the fruition of all his plans.

In business English, the plural **»fruits«** has the meaning of results or revenues. »The fruits of the company's three-year existence were very impressive.«

Train Yourself

1. Setzen Sie die korrekten Formen von »fruit« ein!

1. The project failed after ______ attempts to get it started.
2. The company made a record profit after two very ______ years.
3. After ten years of hard work, we can now sit back and enjoy the ______ of those labours.
4. The plans finally came to ______ after much hard work.
5. I'm glad to hear your efforts were ______ .
6. I told them from the start that their efforts would be in vain and ______ .
7. Their hopes have been realised, they can finally see ______ .
8. I can promise you a ______ visit to our car assembly plant next week.

2. Versuchen Sie dasselbe mit »keep«!

1. I've always avoided dealing with that particularly company, and I'd advise you to keep ______ from them, too.
2. If the company keeps ______ this growth rate next year it will be able to report record profits.
3. If we can only succeed in keeping ______ production costs we shall be able to avoid making a loss.
4. If we keep ______ this course we can't go wrong.
5. Keep those particular salesmen ______ our premises.
6. It's hard work, I know, but try to keep ______ it.
7. Keep it ______ ! You haven't got much further to run.
8. If we want to avoid an accident, we'll have to keep ______ the crowds.

at, away, back, down, off, on, up.

Background Information

Expressions with **»keep«**:

Keep your spirits up!	Cheer up!
Keep your end up!	Don't relax your efforts!

How are you keeping?	How is your health?
keep in good repair	maintain (a home, a car etc.)
keep up appearances	maintain a good appearance
keep in with somebody	remain on good terms with them
keep up your knowledge of something	Are you keeping up your Spanish?
keep up with the Joneses	meaning to work hard at remaining on terms of obvious social equality with the neighbours

Talk Talk Talk

(Marco's restaurant)

(Marcos Restaurant)

J. Well, we certainly have something to celebrate today, Peter. By the way, I've asked Melissa to join us. She had some correspondence of her own to complete and said she'd be along then.

J. Nun, heute haben wir wirklich etwas zu feiern, Peter. Übrigens, ich habe Melissa gebeten, uns Gesellschaft zu leisten. Sie hatte noch einige Korrespondenz zu erledigen und sagte, sie würde danach vorbei kommen.

P. I'm glad to hear that. I do enjoy her company.

P. Freut mich zu hören. Ich mag ihre Gesellschaft.

J. You'll be enjoying more of her company than ever in the weeks ahead. When this new trainee joins us I'd like you to help her acquaint him with the **ins and outs** of marketing – and sales, too, eventually. Steve will also be in on the induction of our new colleague.

J. Sie werden ihre Gesellschaft in den nächsten Wochen öfter denn je genießen. Wenn der neue Trainee zu uns kommt, möchte ich, dass Sie ihr dabei helfen, ihn mit den **Details** des Marketings – und auch des Verkaufs – vertraut zu machen. Steve wird auch bei der Einführung unseres neuen Kollegen dabei sein.

P. Fine, I look forward to it.

P. Schön, ich freue mich schon darauf.

J. I'm sorry to have overloaded you with all that correspondence in the past couple of weeks. I don't know how I allowed it to **accumulate** like that. From now on, it will be a lot easier. I've asked Beryl to give you a hand.

J. Es tut mir Leid, dass ich Sie in den letzten Wochen mit dieser ganzen Korrespondenz so überladen habe. Ich weiß nicht, wie ich zulassen konnte, dass sich das so **ansammelt**. Von jetzt an wird es viel einfacher werden. Ich habe Beryl gebeten, Ihnen zur Hand zu gehen.

P. She's a very willing worker – I get on well with her.

P. Sie ist eine sehr bereitwillige Arbeitskraft, ich komme gut mit ihr aus.

J. Melissa tells me Beryl won't hear a word said against you – not that anyone is. Ah, here's Melissa now ...

J. Melissa sagt, Beryl duldet es nicht, dass auch nur ein schlechtes Wort über Sie gesprochen wird – nicht, dass das einer täte. Ah, da ist Melissa ja ...

Train Yourself

1. Die »ins and outs«!

Die »ins and outs« bedeuten im umgangssprachlichen Englisch die Details von etwas, z.B. eines Dokuments. **Setzen Sie die richtigen Begriffe mit »in« ein!**

1. He couldn't stand his boss and ______ him from the start.
2. She's a very capable worker and ______ to do the job well.
3. Are they ______ the secret?
4. He's really ______ his boss and managed to get two pay rises in one year.
5. I just don't know what's going on - I'm completely ______.
6. Now he has been promoted he is ______.
7. They can't offer us serious competition - they're just not ______.

8. The race will be close-run - there's not much _____ .
9. She dresses well, in clothes that are really _____ .
10. He's _____ big trouble if he tries to evade the tax authorities.

had it in for, has it in her, in clover, in fashion, in it, in on, in the dark, in with, in for, had it in.

2. Zeit zum Üben!
Vervollständigen Sie die folgenden Briefe!

Dear Sirs/Mesdames,

I _____ grateful if you _____ us information _____ your latest products.
_____ we need the information as quickly as _____ , could you please _____ it by _____ post. A complete price list and an explanation of your _____ of payment would also be _____ .

Yours _____ ,
...

Dear Mr Hancock,

With _____ to your letter of February 24, we have _____ in informing you that we have _____ to place an _____ with your company for 60,000 units. Would you please arrange to _____ our stock department to discuss delivery. We would obviously _____ delivery as soon as _____ , and are _____ to meet any extra _____ that this would involve. Invoices should be _____ to our finance department.

Yours _____ ,
...

appreciate, appreciated, contact, costs, decided, express, faithfully, forward, about, order, pleasure, prepared, reference, sent, since, sincerely, terms, would be, possible.

Talk Talk Talk

(Marco's Restaurant)

(Marcos Restaurant)

M. Sorry I'm late. I find it more and more difficult to leave the office at lunch-time these days.

M. Entschuldigung, dass ich zu spät komme. Ich finde es momentan zunehmend schwieriger, das Büro zur Mittagszeit zu verlassen.

J. Anything urgent?

J. Irgendetwas Dringendes?

M. No, not at all, but it would be waiting for me if I **put** it **off** until after lunch. So what has Marco to offer today?

M. Nein, überhaupt nicht, aber es würde auf mich warten, wenn ich es bis nach dem Essen **verschieben würde**. Also, was hat Marco heute anzubieten?

J. I always recommend his gnocchi – but while we're waiting just let's run through the interview procedure. I'm not very good at this. In all my time with the company, I've possibly only hired half a dozen people personally.

J. Ich empfehle immer seine Gnocchi – aber während wir warten, lassen Sie uns noch einmal den Gesprächsablauf durchgehen. Ich bin nicht sehr gut darin. Seit ich für die Firma arbeite, habe ich selbst vielleicht nur ein halbes Dutzend Leute eingestellt.

P. But who did the **hiring**?

P. Aber wer hat die **Einstellungen** übernommen?

J. We used to have a personnel officer – »human resources« officer, I suppose you'd call her these days. When she left we never filled the position.

J. Wir hatten eine Personalbearbeiterin – heutzutage würde man sie wohl »Human Ressources«-Betreuerin nennen. Als sie ging, haben wir die Stelle nicht neu besetzt.

P. So who hires?

P. Wer führt also die Einstellungen durch?

J. You're looking at her right now.	J. Sie sehen sie gerade an.
P. Melissa?	P. Melissa?
J. Yes, but in this case she wants our advice, too – even though the vacancy is in her department. She's being as secretive as ever …	J. Ja, aber in dem Fall möchte sie auch unseren Rat – obwohl die Stelle in ihrer Abteilung frei ist. Sie macht es wie immer geheimnisvoll …

Train Yourself

Im Gespräch erzählt Mr Morgan, dass er schon lange für die Firma arbeitet. Er verwendet dabei den Begriff »to work with«. **»To work« hat noch andere Präpositionen, setzen Sie diese hier ein!**

1. How long have you been working ______ ERGO Limited?
2. I have been working ______ the company for ten years now.
3. He works directly ______ the foreman.
4. I've been working ______ this project for five years.
5. He is a good draughtsman and works ______ great accuracy.
6. She was working ______ Jackson and Partners from 1993 until 1997.
7. Are they working ______ this department?
8. He's working ______ the Dagenham factory.
9. At the moment, I'm working ______ a completely different project.
10. I've been working ______ ERGO Limited one way or another for some time now.
11. He's ______ work on that project at the moment.

at, by, for, in, on, under, with.

Background Information

Further expressions with **»work«**:

a good day's work	a lot has been accomplished, achieved
have one's work cut out	have as much to do as one can manage
give somebody the works	give or tell him or her everything
work away on	continue to work on
work one's fingers to the bone	work very hard
work in	find a place for something
work out	calculate, solve
work off	get rid of

Talk Talk Talk

(Back at the office)

(Zurück im Büro)

S. Oh, Peter, this letter was among my batch today, but I think it's something for you to handle.

S. Ach Peter, der Brief war heute in meinem Stapel, aber ich glaube, Sie sollten sich darum kümmern.

P. Steve, you've **made my day** – my week. I thought I'd got through all the correspondence. But give it here and I'll see what I can do.

P. Steve, Sie haben **meinen Tag gerettet** – meine ganze Woche. Ich dachte, ich wäre mit der gesamten Korrespondenz fertig. Also geben Sie ihn schon her und ich sehe, was ich tun kann.

S. By the way, a few pals and I are playing skittles tonight out in the country, at Farningham. Want to come along?

S. Übrigens, ein paar Kumpel und ich gehen heute zum Kegeln draußen auf dem Land, bei Faringham. Wollen Sie mitkommen?

P. Love to, Steve, but I'm otherwise engaged. Melissa has finally accepted an invitation to dinner.

P. Würde ich liebend gern, Steve, aber ich habe schon was anderes vor. Melissa hat endlich meine Einladung zum Abendessen angenommen.

S. Wow! Watch your step, though, Peter, my friend. She's a man-killer, that one.

S. Wow! Passen Sie auf sich auf, Peter. Die ist eine Männerfresserin.

P. I'll take my chance.

P. Das werde ich riskieren.

S. What can have led her to melt at last?

S. Was hat sie am Ende zum Schmelzen gebracht?

P. Oh, come on Steve, who's talking about melting?

P. Ach kommen Sie schon, Steve, wer redet denn von schmelzen?

(Melissa enters)

(Melissa kommt herein)

M. Who's melting? I am – it's even hotter today than yesterday. Who's going to run out for an ice?

M. Wer schmilzt? Ich schmelze jedenfalls – heute ist es noch heißer als gestern. Wer geht Eis holen?

S. Chip? Chip? Damn me, he's probably sitting on his motorbike right now licking a cornet. OK, you two, choc or vanilla?

S. Chip? Chip? Verdammt noch mal, er sitzt wahrscheinlich gerade auf seinem Motorrad und leckt ein Eis. Okay, ihr beiden, Schoko oder Vanille?

Train Yourself

Peter verwendet den Ausdruck »to take one's chance«. **Vervollständigen Sie die folgenden Sätze mit »take«!**

1. I can't be hurried - this job is going to take ________.
2. Are you tired already? Let's take ________.

3. This is the third time this week she's turned up late - I shall have to take it ______ with her.
4. Take it ______ me, I predict trouble within one month.
5. His qualifications are excellent. He obviously has ______ it takes.
6. The forgery was a very good one. It took us all ______.
7. The finances are in a mess, they need to be taken ______ hand.
8. Did you understand the lecture? Did you take it all ______?
9. He's got a new hobby - he's recently taken ______ collecting antique teapots.
10. I have something important to tell you, but can I really take you ______ my confidence?

The possibilities: a break, from, in, into, time, to, up, what.

Background information

Further expressions with **»take«**:

take for a ride	Deceive (»That swindler took us all for a ride«).
Take it or leave it.	Do as you please.
take it out on	Work off one's frustration by attacking or maltreating another (»He's so unhappy in his job that he takes it out on the dog when he gets home at night«).

Talk Talk Talk

(Peter's office. He opens the letter given to him by Steve …)

(Peters Büro. Er öffnet den Brief von Steve …)

Dear Sirs,

My company is endeavouring to organise a joint exhibit by office software producers and distributors at the upcoming Intertec electronics trade fair. A joint exhibit would reduce costs without necessarily

affecting competitiveness. In fact, we feel a combined stand at the fair would contribute to productive co-operation and a healthy exchange of ideas. A synergy could arise which could be of great benefit to all involved.
I would be very happy to hear your views on this proposal, and would be delighted to answer any questions you may have.

Yours faithfully,

Samuel Trotman,
Chief Executive,
Grant Technologies

(Steve's office. Peter enters)	(Steves Büro. Peter tritt ein)
P. Steve, why did you **pass me on** this letter? It looks like something for Melissa.	P. Steve, warum haben Sie diesen Brief **an mich weitergeleitet**? Sieht aus, als wäre er etwas für Melissa.
S. I'm sorry, Peter, but I'm not in Melissa's **good books** at the moment, and frankly I'm reluctant to drop any work on her desk.	S. Es tut mir Leid, Peter, aber ich stehe bei Melissa im Augenblick **nicht gut im Ansehen** und offen gesagt habe ich Hemmungen, ihr Arbeit auf den Schreibtisch zu legen.
P. OK, I'll be glad to tackle her on it.	P. Also, ich nehme das gerne in Angriff.

Background Information

Business word of the decade is **»Synergy«**. It has long since grown out of its original medicine book context, where it meant the combined effect of medicines that exceeds the sum of their individual effects. In business terms, synergy means the combined positive effect of business co-operation. Two separate companies producing goods or services which can be profitably combined can co-operate and develop a successful synergy.

Train Yourself

Don't pass this by ...

Das Verb »pass« wird oft in geläufigen Ausdrücken verwendet. **Vervollständigen Sie »pass« in den folgenden Sätzen durch die passenden Präpositionen:** *through, up, on, by.*

1. He passed ________ the opportunity to take the company over.
2. The company passed ________ a very difficult phase.
3. He left without passing ________ any of the experience he had gained.
4. Success just passed him ________.
5. Fancy passing ________ a chance like that!
6. They passed ________ without giving us so much as a nod of recognition.

Talk Talk Talk

(Melissa's office. Peter enters)

(Melissas Büro. Peter tritt ein)

P. Hello, Melissa. This letter seems to belong in your department, although I'd be happy to answer it.

P. Hallo Melissa. Dieser Brief scheint in Ihre Abteilung zu gehören, ich kann ihn aber auch gerne beantworten.

M. Let me see (reads the letter). But this is crazy! What can this man Trotman be thinking about? The trade fair arrangements have long since been made. We've booked and paid for our stand – in fact, I've really got to get down to work on preparations for the fair. I really need that assistant – when are we interviewing the candidates?

M. Lassen Sie mich sehen (liest den Brief). Das ist ja verrückt. Was denkt sich dieser Trotham nur? Die Arrangements für die Messe sind schon lange erledigt. Wir haben unseren Stand gebucht und bezahlt, ich muss jetzt wirklich damit anfangen, an den Vorbereitungen für die Messe zu arbeiten. Ich brauche diesen Assistenten wirklich – wann führen wir die

Bewerbungsgespräche mit den Kandidaten?

P. In a couple of weeks' time. It will be about six weeks before you get that help.

P. In ein paar Wochen. In etwa sechs Wochen bekommen Sie Hilfe.

M. Just as the trade fair opens.

M. Genau wenn die Messe öffnet.

P. Well, if there's anything I can do just say the word ...

P. Nun, wenn es irgend etwas gibt, das ich tun kann, sagen Sie es ...

M. Well, reply to that letter, **for starters!**

M. Na ja, beantworten Sie diesen Brief, **für den Anfang**!

Dear Mr Trotman,

Thank you for your letter of August 3. We registered with interest your offer of co-operation in a combined presentation at the forthcoming electronics trade fair. However, we have to inform you that we have already booked our stand-space at the fair, and we shall therefore be exhibiting alone. Nevertheless, we do not rule out co-operation at a suitable level between our companies, and remain open to any proposal from your side.
Wishing Grant Technologies every success at the fair,

Yours faithfully,

Peter Brückner,
Assistant Managing Director

Talk Talk Talk

(Melissa's office. Peter enters and presents her with the letter)

(Melissas Büro. Peter tritt ein und zeigt ihr den Brief)

M. (after reading the letter) Yes, that's fine Peter, thank you.

M. (nachdem sie den Brief gelesen hat) Ja, das ist gut so, Peter, ich danke Ihnen.

P. And that's my last letter for a week. I'm off on holiday tomorrow, Melissa.

P. Und das war mein letzter Brief für eine Woche. Ab morgen bin ich im Urlaub, Melissa.

M. Holiday already?

M. Urlaub, schon?

P. Just a week. I want to have a look at Scotland. I was never there.

P. Nur eine Woche. Ich möchte mir Schottland ansehen. Ich war noch nie dort.

M. You'll be back in time for the interviews?

M. Werden Sie rechtzeitig zu den Bewerbungsgesprächen zurück sein?

P. Yes, of course. I'll be **in** there **at the kill**, as I learnt on my hunting trip!

P. Ja, natürlich. Ich werde **beim Abschuss dabei sein**, wie ich bei meinem Jagdausflug gelernt habe.

Train Yourself

Peter erzählt Melissa, dass er noch nie in Schottland war und verwendet dabei das Simple Past. **Setzen Sie in den folgenden Sätzen das Verb in seiner korrekten Form ein!**

1. I *(live)* in London for four years before moving to Glasgow.
2. I *(live)* in Hamburg now for five years.
3. *(Be)* you ever in Spain?
4. How long *(live)* you in London before moving to Germany?
5. I *(be)* in Paris during that very hot spell of weather.
6. *(spend)* you all your time in the mountains?
7. I *(live)* in Britain all my life.
8. Where *(spend)* you your holidays last year?
9. *(Be)* you ever to Africa?
10. I never *(live)* abroad.

Background Information

Holiday time:

On holiday – »I'm on holiday« - **but**
holidays – »Where will you spend your holidays this year?«
I'm **making** (or **taking**) a holiday from work.
Noun: a holidaymaker.

In American English, vacation is preferred to holiday. »In America, workers usually get two weeks' vacation a year«.
In American English, »vacation« is also a commonly-used verb – »They vacation every year at their beach cottage on Long Island«. »Holiday« is also used as a verb in British English, but not so commonly – »I holidayed in Mallorca last summer«.

Talk Talk Talk

(Two weeks later. James Morgan's office. Morgan, Melissa and Peter sit at a small conference table)	(Zwei Wochen später. James Morgans Büro. Morgan, Melissa und Peter sitzen an einem kleinem Besprechungstisch)
J. Right, how do we go about the selection process? Throw names in a hat? (laughs)	J. Gut, wie treffen wir die Auswahl? Werfen wir die Namen in einen Hut? (lacht)
P. Well, in my view, there's only one person for the job.	P. Also, meiner Meinung nach kommt für die Stelle nur eine Person in Frage.
J. And that is?	J. Und das wäre?
P. No, let's hear what Melissa has to say first.	P. Nein, lassen Sie uns erst hören, was Melissa zu sagen hat.
M. I'm staying out of this first round.	M. Ich setze in der ersten Runde aus.

J. But why? You've been strangely silent from the first.	J. Aber warum? Sie waren von Anfang an merkwürdig still.
M. Please, you two have your say and then I'll add my opinion.	M. Bitte sagen Sie beide erst etwas und dann sage ich meine Meinung dazu.
J. Well, Peter, that's it – who's your prize candidate?	J. Schön, Peter, los geht's – wer ist Ihr Wunschkandidat?
P. Can I make a suggestion? We all write the name of our preference on a slip of paper and then **disclose** our choices.	P. Kann ich einen Vorschlag machen? Wir schreiben alle den Namen der von uns bevorzugten Person auf ein Blatt Papier und **verdecken** unsere jeweilige Wahl.
J. Is this a German practice? Sounds like a betting syndicate to me. But I don't mind. All right with you, Melissa?	J. Ist das eine deutsche Vorgehensweise? Klingt für mich wie eine Wette. Aber mir soll es recht sein. Sind Sie einverstanden, Melissa?
M. On just one condition – that my selection is read last of all.	M. Unter einer Bedingung – dass meine Wahl als Letzte vorgelesen wird.
J. The suspense is killing me, but that's all right by me. Pencil and paper?	Die Spannung bringt mich um, aber ich bin einverstanden. Papier und Bleistift?

Train Yourself

Peter Brückner schlägt vor, den richtigen Bewerber auszulosen und verwendet dabei den Begriff »disclose«. »Dis-« ist eine weit verbreitete Vorsilbe, die Substantiven, Adjektiven und Verben viele verschiedene Bedeutungen verleihen kann. Einerseits kann es sich hierbei um eine Unterscheidung von Etwas zu etwas Anderem handeln (»distinguish«), aber auch um ein Gegenteil oder die Umkehrung einer Handlung (»disable, dishonest«). **Finden Sie nun in den folgenden Sätzen die richtige Form!**

1. The trade union is not represented in that factory – the workers are totally ______ .
2. The company ______ all responsibility for the late deliveries.
3. We ______ ourselves from his actions.
4. The management showed its ______ by cancelling the usual holiday bonus.
5. The strike action ______ production at the assembly plant.
6. He's a liar and a cheat, in fact an utterly ______ person.
7. The projects manager ______ all our ideas, he just ignored them.
8. We have a very generous expense allowance at our ______ .
9. The entire board of directors was ______ at the annual meeting.
10. The ______ workers threatened strike action.
11. The office is in a completely ______ state, with papers all over the place.
12. He's a very ______ worker, with no system or routine.
13. The firm ______ after trying for three years to recover its losses.
14. The factory was sold off and then ______ piece by piece.
15. There's no ______ in admitting you made a mistake.
16. The supporters were very ______ by their side's defeat in the Cup.

disadvantaged, disclaimed, disgruntled, disheartened, dishonour, disintegrated, dismantled, dismissed, disorderly, disorganised, displeasure, disposal, disregarded, disreputable, disrupted, dissociated.

Talk Talk Talk

(James Morgan's office)	(James Morgans Büro)
J. Right, where are the slips of paper? Let's see what name is on yours, Peter! Good heavens! Martin Russell!	J. Gut, wo sind die Zettel? Lassen Sie uns sehen, welcher Name auf Ihrem steht, Peter! Gütiger Himmel! Martin Russell!

P. Why the surprise?

P. Warum die Überraschung?

J. That's the young man I've chosen, too. Whose name is on your slip of paper, Melissa? Here with it! But you've written nothing down. No name at all. What does that mean?

J. Das ist der junge Mann, den ich auch gewählt habe. Wessen Name ist auf Ihrem Zettel, Melissa? Her damit! Aber Sie haben ja nichts hingeschrieben. Überhaupt keinen Namen. Was soll das bedeuten?

M. But since you two have **unanimously** chosen Martin Russell, my choice is **immaterial**.

M. Nachdem Sie beide **einstimmig** Martin Russel gewählt haben, ist meine Wahl **bedeutungslos**.

J. That's not true, you'll be working with him, Melissa.

J. Das ist nicht wahr, Melissa, Sie werden mit ihm zusammenarbeiten.

M. I'll have no problem at all working with young Martin Russell.

M. Ich werde keinerlei Schwierigkeiten haben, mit dem jungen Martin Russel zusammenzuarbeiten.

J. You know him?

J. Sie kennen ihn?

M. I have met him on a few occasions, yes. He's Beryl's nephew. That's why I had to withdraw from the final selection process. But since you two have both **plumped for** Martin it didn't make much difference, did it?

M. Ja, ich habe ihn bei ein paar Gelegenheiten getroffen. Er ist Beryls Neffe. Deswegen musste ich mich vom endgültigen Auswahlprozess zurückziehen. Aber nachdem Sie beide für Martin **gestimmt** haben, machte das keinen großen Unterschied, nicht wahr?

J. Well, I'll be damned. You're good for surprises, Melissa.

J. Ja, verflucht noch mal. Sie sind für Überraschungen gut, Melissa.

M. Can I go and tell Beryl? She'll be delighted. And you'll be delighted with Martin on the staff, too. He'll be a credit to ERGO!

M. Kann ich gehen und es Beryl erzählen? Sie wird begeistert sein. Und Sie werden begeistert sein, Martin als Angestellten zu haben. Er wird ein Gewinn für ERGO sein!

Train Yourself

Melissa erwähnt, dass ihre Wahl »immaterial« (nicht wichtig) ist, also »not material«. **Setzen Sie die richtigen Negativpräfixe »un«, »in« oder »im« in den folgenden Sätzen ein:**

1. I find it extremely ______polite to smoke while others are eating.
2. The union's wage demands were ______moderate.
3. I find his remarks quite ______appropriate.
4. We could hardly understand a thing he said - he's very ______articulate.
5. Mozart's music made him ______mortal.
6. No, it can't be changed. It's ______alterable.
7. She won't forgive me - she's quite ______placable.
8. I won't accept such behaviour. It's quite ______tolerable.
9. The company president is totally ______pervious to such arguments.
10. The damage he did to the company is ______measurable.

Vocabulary

to accumulate	ansammeln
to disclose	verdecken
to draft	entwerfen
for starters	für den Anfang
to hire	einstellen
in black and white	schwarz auf weiß
ins and outs	alle Details
in somebody's good books	bei jemandem gut im Ansehen stehen
immaterial	bedeutungslos
to make sb.'s day	einem den Tag retten
to plump for	stimmen für
to put off	verschieben
short-list	Auswahlliste
to shift through	durchschauen
to sink	ruinieren
to whittle down	reduzieren

The Test – how good are you now in writing?

1. Sie haben eine Liste mit Leuten, denen Sie Briefe oder E-Mails schreiben müssen. **Wie beginnen und beenden Sie Ihre Briefe?**

a. To Mr Smith, General Manager of Acorn Foods? __________ ... __________.

b. To your good friend John Trebbit? __________ ... __________.

c. To the Management of Callout Electronics? __________ ... __________.

d. To Rosemary Charles, Chairlady of the Society of American Women for World Action? __________ ... __________.

e. An email to Donald Higgins, a colleague? __________ ... __________.

f. To the General Manager, Sun Hotels? __________ ... __________.

2. Ihre Marketing-Abteilung erhält den folgenden Brief. **Wie entwerfen Sie ein Antwortschreiben?**

Manchester, 28 July, 2007
Dear Sirs,

We would be very grateful if you sent us the fullest information you have on your range of products, including price list, delivery terms and dates and guarantee details. Are you able to arrange with our Mr Jones a suitable time and place for a meeting to discuss the possibility of further co-operation between our two companies? We look forward to your reply.

Yours faithfully,
Thompson and Partners

3. Wird der folgende Brief dem Schreiber den gewünschten Job bescheren, was meinen Sie? **Können Sie ihn für ihn verbessern?**

Dear gentlemen,

I have read with a lot of interest the announcement you positioned in the newspaper of last week seeking an office assistant. I have much experience of office and I sure I might be the man you require. Up to now I work as stores manager of Hancock and Sons, just round corner from you – very convenient! I work in stores but often in office, so I know way around. My English not yet very good but I try to learn more. I make 300 pounds the week. You offer me me I your man.

With many greetings,

...

4. *Write* or *draft*? *Type up* or *take down*? **Setzen Sie die richtigen Formen in die folgenden Sätze ein.**

a. Miss Manners, would you please bring in your notebook and pencil and ________ a letter for me?

b. I ________ them a letter of complaint, but I did it in the heat of the moment and I should have ________ it first and then looked at it again the next day.

c. Miss Manners, would you please ________ that letter as soon as possible. I promised Hatcher and Company we would ________ to them today.

d. Just __________ the version you want to send and I'll get Miss Manners to __________ the letter.

e. Before you __________ that letter __________ this version first, and then __________ it __________. If there are any additions I'll just __________ them in.

1. Geschäftsbriefe

Stil und Layout

Your Ref: ...
Our Ref: ...

Date: September 19, 2007

Miller Machines Inc.
Attn: Mr Anthony Brown (*oder* Anthony Brown)
Purchasing Manager
5 Newton Street
Newport, Gwent

Dear Mr Brown,

Your enquiry dated April 4, 2007

Thank you for your letter of April 4, 2007 and the interest you showed in our products (...)

(...)

We enclose the requested company brochure and various catalogues. We hope that we have made you a favourable offer and look forward to hearing from you.

Sincerely,

Doris Smith
Export Sales Manager

Anrede

Dear Sir,	Sehr geehrter Herr ...,
Dear Madam,	Sehr geehrte Frau ...,
Dear Sir/Madam,	Sehr geehrte Damen und Herren,
Dear Mr (Mrs/Ms) Norman,	Sehr geehrter Herr/Frau Norman,
Dear Andrew,	Lieber Andrew,

Sirs, (distanziert)

Einleitende Phrasen

Thank you for your inquiry of May 4.

Thank you for your letter of May 14.
= We acknowledge receipt of your letter of ... /
We are in receipt of your letter of ... (very formal)
Thank you for your letter of ..., to which we now have pleasure in replying positively.

I regret to have to inform you that ...

I am writing to inquire if ...

We are writing to compliment your company on ...

Subsequent to our letter of June 6 ... (after sending you our letter of)

Schlussformeln

We have great pleasure in enclosing complete information on ...

Should you have any further questions or require additional information do not hesitate to contact me on my personal extension.

Ms Norman asks me to add her sincere greetings.

Looking forward to hearing from you,
Yours sincerely,

Hoping to hear from you forthwith / soon,

Assuring you of our best attention at all times,
Yours sincerely,

Thanking you in advance for your prompt
attention to this matter,
Yours faithfully,
Mr Brückner joins me in sending greetings,

We remain, ... (distanziert)

Grußformeln

Yours sincerely,	Mit freundlichen Grüßen
Yours faithfully,	Mit freundlichen Grüßen
Yours truly,	Mit freundlichen Grüßen
Sincerely,	Mit freundlichen Grüßen
Best regards,	Mit freundlichen Grüßen
Kind regards,	Mit herzlichem Gruß
With kindest regards	Herzliche Grüße/ Mit herzlichen Grüßen

Abkürzungen

Encl.	Anlage
c.c.	Kopie an
Attn:	zu Händen von
dd (dated)	datiert
p.p.	i.A/i.V./ppa.

Bewerbungsschreiben

I noted with interest your advertisement for an Assistant Managing Director in today's Morning Post.
My attention was caught by your company's insertion in the Morning Echo, advertising the vacancy in your Marketing Department.

I am available under the above address and telephone number to provide additional information.

Antworten auf Bewerbungsschreiben

We acknowledge receipt of your application for the position which has become available in our Marketing Department, and we have pleasure in inviting you for an interview.

Following your application for the position of Assistant Marketing Officer, we have pleasure in inviting you to an interview next week.

We look forward very much to meeting you,
Yours sincerely,

Beispiel für einen Lebenslauf

Name:
Address:
Telephone number:
Email:

Born:

Education
Primary :
Secondary:
Certificates:

Universities:
Additional studies and work experience:

References can be obtained from:

Vergessen Sie nicht das Datum und Ihre Unterschrift!

2. Faxmitteilungen

Mittlerweile ist auch in Großbritannien eine knappe Formulierung in Faxen weit verbreitet und akzeptiert. Die Formalia, die in Briefen zutreffen, sind daher nicht zwingend und können in einem Fax zu Gunsten einer kurzen, präzisen Formulierung aufgegeben werden.

FAX MESSAGE

Hans Müller GmbH
Seestraße 7
D 28717 Bremen

TO: Mr Mike Williams
Clark Industries

FROM: Mr Robert Wagner

DATE: September 19, 2007

Ref.: Conference

Dear Mr Williams,
We can attend the conference between the above dates. Please send details of accommodation and itinerary.
Thanks and regards,
Robert Wagner

Übertragungsfehler

Please refax.	Bitte noch einmal faxen.
Please repeat transmission.	Bitte Übertragung wiederholen.
The first transmission was difficult	Die erste Übertragung war schwer leserlich.
Someone using this fax number tried to fax us this morning.	Jemand mit dieser Faxnummer hat heute Morgen versucht uns zu faxen.
Our fax machine ran out of paper.	Unser Faxgerät hatte kein Papier mehr.
Please resend.	Bitte schicken Sie es noch einmal.

3. E-Mails

In Großbritannien und in den USA werden E-Mails in einem sehr viel informelleren Stil als in Deutschland geschrieben. Beispielsweise ist es üblich, den Adressaten mit Vornamen anzusprechen und sich informell zu verabschieden.

Re: Marketing concept
Date: 18 September 2007
From: viertill@gdf.bav.de
To: wyattjl@dds.bham.uk

Hi Jeremy,
Many thanks for your mail which I received yesterday.
I have taken into account the changes you suggested and have attached, in simple text format, what I would suggest should be the final draft of the marketing concept for your new range of products.

If you have any problems reading the attachment, please let us know and we can fax the relevant documents to you.

I look forward to hearing from you soon,
Till

Glossary

accounting program	Buchführungsprogramm
to accumulate	ansammeln
to advertise a post	eine Stelle annoncieren
to attend to	bearbeiten
to affect	beeinflussen
appendix, appendices (pl.)	Anhang
to assign	unterzeichnen
batch	Stoß
to bring out	herausbringen
berk	Dussel/Idiot (umgangssprachlich)
to bin	wegwerfen
to blind sb. with science	jdn. mit großen Worten beeindrucken
blunder	(schwerer) Fehler
boast	prahlen (hier: etwas vorweisen können)
to break off	aufhören/abbrechen
brief	kurz
bundle	Bündel/Packen
to buzz about	umhersausen
business-related discipline	wirtschaftliches Ausbildungsfach
to check out	nachgehen
catch up on letter-writing	überfällige Briefe schreiben
to chuck	zerknüllen
complaint	Beschwerde
confirmation	Bestätigung
considerable	beachtlich
to couch	formulieren, »sprachlich einbetten«
devoted to	gewidmet
degree in economics	Abschluss in Wirtschaftswissenschaft
dictaphone	Diktiergerät
to disclose	verdecken
to draft	entwerfen

to end a letter	einen Brief beenden
dire	gräßlich/hier: weitreichend, unangenehm
discipline	hier: Fachgebiet
to divert	ablenken
do the trick	funktionieren
dog-tired	hundemüde
dying to	»sterben« etwas zu sehen/ hören etc.
to entail	beinhalten/nach sich ziehen
effect	Auswirkung
to fall into	hinein fallen (im Sinne von dazu gehören)
fine by me	ist mir Recht
for all the tea in China	(Redewendung), etwa: Für alles Geld der Welt
forceful	hier: ausgeprägt (Charakter)
formal	formell
for starters	für den Anfang
foxed	verblüfft
(to be) geared up	bereit sein (etwa: seine Sieben Sachen zusammen haben)
to get the better of	etwas nachgeben, nichts widerstehen können
franchise	Franchise
generously-proportioned	großzügig geschnitten
to get through	durchkriegen
to give a telling off	eine Standpauke halten
grey zone	Grauzone
to have bigger fish to fry	einen größeren Fisch am Haken haben (etwas Wichtigeres vorhaben)
head office	Hauptbüro
highly desirable	höchst attraktiv
to hire	einstellen
het-up	aufgeregt/erhitzt über etwas
hype	zielgerichtete Übertreibung/ »Hype«

immaterial	bedeutungslos
in a jiffy	im Handumdrehen/in «Windeseile«
in a state	hier: in einem schlechten Zustand sein
in black and white	schwarz auf weiß
to inquire about	sich erkundigen nach
in the meantime	in der Zwischenzeit
in the picture	im Bild sein/Bescheid wissen
incompatible	unverträglich/unvereinbar
indisposed	unpässlich (hier: unabkömmlich)
initial	anfänglich
inquiry	Anfrage
ins and outs	alle Details
in sb.'s good books	bei jdm. gut im Ansehen stehen
in-tray	(Post-) Eingangskorb
to junk	wegwerfen
to keep abreast of	Schritt halten mit
to keep sb. posted	auf dem Laufenden halten/ informieren
job inquiry	Bewerbung
to make sb.'s day	einem den Tag retten
to make up a file	einen Ordner anlegen
letter-head	Briefkopf
look-see	kurzer Blick
lousy	lausig, verflixt
make it snappy	machen Sie schnell/fix
to make up lost time	verlorene Zeit aufholen
market exposure	Markteinführung
to meet one's match	seinen Meister treffen
marketing push	Marketing-Initiative
missive	Mitteilung
to narrow down	eingrenzen
not to cry over spilt milk	»was passiert ist, ist passiert«
off-base	außerhalb (einer Firma etc.)
offhand	unpersönlich
on file	in den Unterlagen
on occasion	bei Gelegenheit

on the spot	vor Ort
on the turn	sofort, umgehend
open-and-shut	klar und deutlich/eindeutig
opening	freie Stelle
out-tray	(Post-)Ausgangskorb
papers	Unterlagen
per capita	pro Kopf
permanent location	ständiger Wohnsitz
to plump for	stimmen für
to put off	verschieben, hinhalten
pick-you-up	Muntermacher
to propagate	verbreiten
push	Initiative/Vorstoß (bes. im Marketing)
to put into practice	in die Praxis umsetzen
to rectify	richtig stellen
range of products	Produktpalette
to reply to	beantworten
referral	Vermittlung
refrain from	sich zurückhalten
to regret	bedauern
request	Anfrage
requirements	Anforderungen
retail (trade)	Einzelhandel
retrenchment	Einschränkung/Kürzung; Kostenreduzierung
to rubbish	mies/schlecht machen
sales director	Verkaufsleiter
»sell-by« date	Haltbarkeitsdatum
to sort out	aussortieren
short-list	Auswahlliste
to shift through	durchschauen
to sink	ruinieren
some of the leads	ein paar der Wichtigsten
(a) stack of	ein ganzer Haufen (von)
stacks	Stapel (hier: «stapelweise««)
stiff	steif (hier: rau, umkämpft)
stinker	harter Brocken

stock	Vorrat
to store	abspeichern
streamlining	Leistungssteigerung
strike from	ausstreichen/herausnehmen
to stuck into sth.	sich in etwas vertiefen/ «hineinknien«
to subcontract	Unteraufträge vergeben
submerged in letters	unter einem Briefberg begraben
to take a letter	einen Brief aufnehmen
to take if from here	jetzt weiter vorgehen
to tackle some letters	ein Paar Briefe durchgehen
to type up	abtippen
urge	inständig bitten, drängen
to whitle down	reduzieren
subtle	subtil/feinsinnig
to swot (colloquial)	«büffeln«, »pauken« (umgangssprachlich)
tabular	tabellarisch
to take it	annehmen
to tend to	dazu tendieren/neigen
testimonial	Anerkennung/(positive) Referenz
(to be) tied down	in etwas eingebunden sein
unconditionally	bedingungslos/ohne Vorbehalte
user-friendly	benutzerfreundlich
well-worded	wohl formuliert
work up a thirst	sich durstig arbeiten
writer's cramp	Schreibkrampf
zilch	Nichts (umgangssprachlich)

Solutions

Seite

8. 1. Yours sincerely; 2. Yours faithfully; 3. With best wishes; 4. Yours sincerely; 5. Yours sincerely; 6. With best wishes; 7. Yours faithfully; 8. Yours sincerely.

12. 1: request; 2: request; 3: demand; 4: refusal; 5: rejection; 6: denial; 7: withholding; 8: offer.

15. grateful; sent; range; products; products; developed; employ; areas; operations; scheduled; useful; arrange; reply; faithfully.

17. 1: banned; 2: seen; 3: several times; 4: start work; 5: stop; 6: land.

18. 1. cause; inform; defence; unaware; in question; prohibiting; assumed; used; refrain; opportunity; appeal; vicinity.
2. b; c.

22. has written; to complain; promised; to explain; has not turned up; tells; had suspended; looked at; says; decided to give; to call; had not done so; would strike; look.

23. 1: attractive; 2: site; 3: has; 4: large; 5: recommend.

26. 1: have written; 2: write; 3: will write; 4: written; 5: write; 6: wrote; 7: am writing.

28. receipt; prompt; appreciate; early; assured; best; reply; grateful; sent.

31. clearer; more brief; longer; more legible; more insulting; lengthier; sooner.

33. Dear Mr Green,
Thank you again for your invitation to lunch, which I originally very gratefully accepted. However, a very urgent business engagement has in the meantime cropped up and upset my plans. I regretfully have to cancel my plan to join you for lunch. Please excuse any inconvenience this might cause. I hope I may make amends and reciprocate by inviting you to lunch at the earliest opportunity.

With best regards,
...

Cropped up? *To crop up* means to occur unexpectedly.

38. 1: c, b; 2: c, c; 3: c, b; 4: c, a.

42. 1: personal; 2: personal, personal; 3: Personal, personnel; 4: recommendation; 5: referrals; 6: referral.

45. My company was told to put the order in more than a month ago and we were kept waiting until today for delivery. The package was delivered by the courier service during the lunch break, so its contents could not be checked immediately. When the package was opened by our sorting department it was discovered that the wrong product had been sent by ATCO. The sorting department was instructed to contact you without delay, but your dispatch department insisted that the correct item had been sent.

46. 1: commission, rebates; 2: rebate, commission; 3: commission, rebate.

48. 1: having; 2: objecting; 3: Before objecting; 4: am writing to inform; 5: After informing ... ready to sign (or ready for signing); 6: in informing ... to collect; 7: In ordering, to give; 8: to order, to be delivered; 9: Before ordering; 10; contacting; 11: Before contacting; 12: to contact.

50. malfunction, question, delay, send, fail to observe, eliminate mistake, examine, usually, furious, job, put together, disguise, at once.

52. 1. acknowledge, apologise, regrettable, dispatching, in time, lay, arrival, parts, suppliers, lodged, hope, discount, pass, apologizing, inconvenience, assuring, faithfully.
2. 1: early; 2: disappointed; 3: receive; 4: reply; 5: insincere; 6: mistrust; 7: right; 8: easy; 9: fail; 10; forget; 11: depart.

57. 1: testimonial; 2: recommendation; 3: testimonial.

59. PRO; PR; p.a.; pro tem; p/e; p.c.; PS

62. 1: therefore; 2: nevertheless; 3: therefore; 4: nevertheless; 5: therefore.

64. 1. An article on your company's software program, »Instantweb«, which the American magazine Computer World carried, has caught our attention ... This possibility particularly interested our Head Office in the United States, which has asked us to approach you with a view to obtaining the franchise for »Instantweb« in the United States.
2. 1: but; 2: and; 3: because; 4: since; 5: but; 6: and.

66. 1. 1: price; 2: price; 3: costs; 4: prices, costs; 5: price, costs, prices; 6: price, cost.
2. 1: consequences; 2: consequently; 3: Consequent; 4: consequently.

69. 1: basic facts; 2: information; 3: examine; 4: inside information; 5: inform; 6: essence.

71. 1: a; 2: c; 3: h; 4: b; 5: e; 6: f; 7: d; 8: g.

74. 1: b; 2: a; 3: c.

76. 1: convenient, expect; 2: mark, inviting, reception; 3: glad, invitation; 4: kind, attend, pleased; 5: honour, company; 6: afraid; 7: engaged.

78. 1. 1: any; 2: any; 3: some; 4: any; 5: any; 6: some; 7: any, some; 8: some.
2. 1: something; 2: anything; 3: something; 4: anything; 5: something; 6: anything; 7: anything; 8: something.

80. 1: Before replying: 2: after reading; 3: During ... to reply; 4: after receiving; 5: Before agreeing; 6: After examining, meanwhile; 7: During, has learnt; 8: Before leaving; 9: while ... are waiting; 10: After studying.

83. 1: effect; 2: affect; 3: effect; 4: affect; 5: effect; 6: effect; 7: effects; 8: affect; 9: effect; 10: effects.

85. Dear Sirs/Mesdames,

Thank you for your interest in our new product and your request for information. We are pleased to be able to send you our latest information on the product, and will be happy to answer any further inquiries you may have ...

Alternativen zum zweiten Satz: We have pleasure in sending you our latest information ...; We are glad to be able to send you our latest information ...

87. 1: patiently; 2: immediate; 3: fully; 4: promptly; 5: complete; 6: necessarily; 7: usually, prompt; 8: completely; 9: fully; 10: Happily; 11: patiently; 12: unusually; 13: badly; 14: Bad.

89. 1: in; 2: at, as; 3: by; 4: up; 5: down; 6: up; 7: into; 8: out; 9: at, for; 10: around.

92. 1: break; 2: have been broken; 3: break-in; 4: break up; 5: broken; 6: has broken away; 7: broken up; 8: broken out.

94. 1: to accept; 2: of telling; 3: of reading; 4: to deliver; 5: of being; 6: to see; 7: of paying; 8: to make.

96. was born; attending; left; took; travelled; returning; enrolled; completing; joined; gained; am employed; is; am studying; includes maintaining; organizing; has taken; feel.

99. 1: impressed by; 2: impressive; 3: impressively; 4: impression, on; 5: impressive; 6: impressed by; 7: to impress; 8: an impression on; 9: impressively; 10: impressed by.

101. 1: certify; 2: admit; 3: confirm; 4: accepted; 5: recognised; 6: accepted; 7: admitted; 8: avowed.

103. 1: whom; 2: whose; 3: Whom; 4: who; 5: who; 6: Who; 7: Whose; 8: whom; 9: who; 10: whose.

105. 1: of ... interest; 2: interesting; 3: interested in; 4: interest ... by; 5: interesting; 6: interest; 7: interest to; 8: interested; 9: interesting; 10: interested in; 11: interest; 12: interesting.

106. 1: I only wanted to meet her before she left. Now it's too late.
2: They should be only too pleased they didn't take up that offer.
3: I'm only too grateful for the help you gave me.
4: It's not only the anger it causes, but also the pain.
5: We've only two miles to go before we get home.
6: I shall be only too glad to do that for you.

108. 1: mispronounce; 2: mischance; 3: misanthrope; 4: misshapen; 5: misspend; 6: miscellany; 7: misdirect; 8: misgiving; 9: misfit; 10: misdeed; 11: misconduct; 12: misnomer.

110. 1: incapable; 2: impervious; 3: unable; 4: disproportionate; 5: abnormal; 6: insensitive; 7: impassively; 8: unaffected; 9: unstable; 10: insecure; 11: unseemly; 12: ungracious; 13: illegible; 14: unhealthy; 15: intolerable; 16: uncertain.

114. 1: by; 2: on; 3: into; 4: in; 5: up; 6: with; 7: down; 8: along; 9: out; 10: over; 11: under; 12: across.

116. 1: on; 2: through; 3: into; 4: down; 5: off; 6: through; 7: around; 8: out; 9: there; 10: into; 11: down; 12: back; 13: together; 14: round.

120. 1.1: fruitless; 2: fruitful; 3: fruits; 4: fruition; 5: fruitful; 6: fruitless; 7: fruit; 8: fruitful
2.1: away; 2: up; 3: down; 4: on; 5: away from; 6: at; 7: up; 8: back.

122. 1.1: had it in for; 2: had it in; 3: in on; 4: in with; 5: in the dark; 6: in clover; 7: in it; 8: in it; 9: in fashion; 10: in for.

2. would be; sent; about; since; possible; forward; express; terms; appreciated; faithfully.
reference; pleasure; decided; order; contact; appreciate; possible; prepared; costs; sent; sincerely.

125. 1: at; 2: with; 3: under; 4: in; 5: with; 6: at; 7: in; 8: at; 9: on; 10: with; 11: at.

127. 1: time; 2: a break; 3: up; 4: from; 5: what; 6: in; 7: in; 8: in; 9: to; 10: into.

130. 1: up; 2: through; 3: on; 4: by; 5: up; 6: by.

132. 1: lived; 2: have been living; 3: Were; 4: did you live; 5: was; 6: Do you spend; 7: have lived; 8: did you spend; 9: Have you ever been; 10: have never lived.

134. 1: disgruntled; 2: disclaimed; 3: dissociated; 4: displeasure; 5: disrupted; 6: disreputable; 7: disregarded; 8: disposal; 9: dismissed; 10: disadvantaged; 11: disorderly; 12: disorganised; 13: disintegrated; 14: dismantled; 15: dishonour; 16: disheartened.

137. 1: im; 2: im; 3: in; 4: in; 5: im; 6: un; 7: im; 8: in; 9: im; 10: im.

Lösung zum Abschlusstest:

1. a. Dear Mr Smith. Yours sincerely.
b. Dear John. Best regards.
c. Dear Mesdames/Sirs. Yours faithfully.
d. Dear Ms Charles. Yours sincerely.
e. Dear Donald. Yours truly.
f. Dear Sir. Yours faithfully.

2. Musterentwurf:
Dear Sirs,

Thank you for your letter of 28 July. We have pleasure in enclosing the latest and fullest information on our range of products, together with the additional material you requested: price list, delivery terms and dates and guarantee details. We would be pleased to arrange a meeting with Mr Jones at his convenience to discuss the possibility of further co-operation between our two companies.

Yours faithfully,

3. Musterentwurf:
Dear Sirs,

I read with interest your insertion in last week's newspaper advertising the vacant post of office assistant, and I would be grateful if you considered my application for the job. I am currently employed by Hancock and Sons as store manager, but my employment here has given me the opportunity to acquaint myself with office routine. My salary with Hancock and Sons is 300 pounds a week. Although my English is not yet fluent I am learning the language and hope to gain proficiency soon.

Yours faithfully,

4. a. take down; b. wrote, drafted; c. type up, write; d. draft, type up; e. write, take down, type ... up, write.